"ME AND I'M GREAT"
Physical Education
for Children
Three through Eight

Susan Dimond Block

University of Bridgeport
Bridgeport, Connecticut

photographs by
Don Perrelli

Burgess Publishing Company
Minneapolis, Minnesota

Consulting Editors to the Publisher

Eloise M. Jaeger
University of Minnesota
Minneapolis, Minnesota

Robert M. Clayton
Colorado State University
Fort Collins, Colorado

Book design and drawings by Paula Gibbons.

Copyright © 1977 by Burgess Publishing Company
Printed in the United States of America
Library of Congress Catalog Card Number 76-24334
ISBN: 0-8087-2801-6

0 9 8 7 6 5 4 3 2 1

Dedication

Men who are loving help their
women bloom.

To my husband, Joel; my sons,
Ivan and Eric; my father, Albert.

About the Author:

Susan Dimond Block teaches Parent-Child Physical Education at Yale University and undergraduate elementary physical education classes at Arnold College, University of Bridgeport, Connecticut. She also specializes in adult fitness at the Cheshire YMCA, Cheshire, Connecticut. Mrs. Block has her M.S. in Phy. Ed. and is working toward her doctorate in administration and supervision. She frequently lectures on the aspects of early childhood physical education, has made a television appearance, and has published numerous articles on the same area of expertise. Mrs. Block is the mother of two young boys and the wife of a science teacher and writer.

Contents

Author's Note:
For the purposes of the text children are referred to in the masculine and teachers regarded in the feminine. *By no means* does the author wish to convey any discrimination based on sex. We are *people* first, and this is the primary concept to remember when reading *Me and I'm Great*.

Preface

This guide for early childhood physical education is the result of the writer's experience in YMCA, day care, elementary and secondary school, and university work. The programs taught have been personally planned and organized to use home-made equipment and a minimal amount of supplies. The lack of information available to the public has been the incentive for this guide.

Bodily awareness for children is one of the most important areas in education today. Sadly enough, it is often overlooked. What the writer will show is the *how* and *why* of physical education for the young child. Day care centers, nursery schools, kindergartens, recreational centers, and parents interested in the motor development of their children have very few written materials to turn to.

Many people assume that youngsters are born with the knowledge of things adults take for granted. But they are not! Almost everything a child does must be learned through formal education, example, experience, or maturation. For example, a simple thing such as the command *walk forward* is totally confusing to a child. He has never been taught what *forward* means. Telling him that it is the opposite of *backward* solves nothing, because he doesn't know the meaning of *opposite* or *backward*. Recognition of achievement and the development of self-confidence are two of the crucial areas reinforced in the early childhood physical education program that have carry-over value for the rest of a youngster's life. It is our obligation as educators and parents to make such a program a necessity rather than a luxury.

This guide will attempt to correlate the psychological and motor development of young children, to show the importance of physical education to their growth, and to outline a complete program of activities ranging from apparatus work to games and stunts.

The book is organized to progress from the simple to the more complex skills. Movement exploration, since much of it is based on personal creativity, will be the easiest and most relaxed activity with which to introduce the program. Basic rhythmic movements are next in order of difficulty. These provide a good foundation on which to build. The section on fitness calls for more structure along with the development of agility, flexibility, and coordination. The book continues in complexity, ending with the most difficult of areas, relay racing. Here the child learns to complete an individual skill as well as to work with his peers. It should be noted that many of the photographs were taken in the classroom to show the applicability of activities in limited space.

This book is also designed as a guide to enhance the talents of the individual teacher. Each chapter contains a myriad of suggestions from which the reader may choose what he or she desires given the uniqueness and age of each class. It should be noted that no two youngsters are alike. The method of handling a class must be left up to the discretion of the instructor. It is also necessary to realize that no two teachers are alike. Much of the approach to early childhood physical education will be trial and error. There are no hard and fast rules except those of safety. It is not only the child's readiness and personal needs that will ultimately determine the degree of success attained in the program, but also the instructor's enthusiasm and imagination. If the reader can remember that the main objective is to help create self-confident and happy children, then the goals will have been reached!

I wish to express deep appreciation for the encouragement and enthusiasm shown by the parents of my students at the Cheshire YMCA, Cheshire, Connecticut; the parents and children at Yale; and the children from Hamden Hall Country Day

School. A special thanks is extended to Dr. T. Erwin Blesh, whose assistance was invaluable.

Appreciation also goes to Pat Dixon, Jean Wadley, Loretta Hoey, and Nina Greenwood for their typing expertise and to the numerous friends, especially Ruth Conger Kapodistrias, who made my manuscript a part of their lives. The photographs were taken by Germain Studios, Cheshire, Connecticut and by Donald Perelli, Assistant Athletic Director, Southern Connecticut State College. I wish to acknowledge a special debt of gratitude to Donald Perrelli for his sensitive pictures of my children.

The most deserving of recognition is my husband, Joel. Without his faith in my dream, constant encouragement, and incredible patience, this book might never have been written.

Fall 1976   S.D.B.

Chapter 1

The Young Child: What He Is All About

The young child is a complex little person. He is extremely clever, perceives the world with far more wisdom than we realize, and is totally honest in his reactions and feelings. Anyone with a three-year-old can validate that statement. Just ask a parent who has hit another car in a parking lot and has tried to keep it from the spouse. The three-year-old will go into great detail about how the "accident" occurred, the size of the dent, and the policeman's uniform.

In order to help the young child achieve his potentialities, we must know as much as possible about his emotional needs, mental capacity, and physical ability. A successful physical education program will utilize this information and incorporate it into a complete, sound learning experience.

THE HOW AND WHY OF LEARNING

For the young child, movement is the very essence of existence. He learns about his relationship to space; he learns to deal with problem solving and decision making, to follow directions, to work with his peers, to enhance creative ability, and to discover what he is all about. The young child utilizes movement as a means to an end rather than as an end in itself. Teaching a youngster simply results will never develop creative thinking nor exploratory options. Through movement he can learn indirectly the *how* and the *why* for all his actions.

The young child who is learning to move is constantly experimenting, exploring, making decisions, and creating in accordance with his present and past experiences. Moving is the very essence of play.

Through play a child learns socialization, direction-following, and the development of motor and language skills. His exposure broadens, and through this comes the opportunity to try new and exciting skills. The child's sense of autonomy is strengthened, and he develops self-confidence through having his efforts positively reinforced. Through movement play, the young child will develop interests and preferences as he matures.[1]

Since the purpose of this book is to serve as a guide to early childhood physical education, this writer does not go into detail about perceptual-motor learning, sensorimotor learning, nor cognitive development. If the reader is interested in pursuing these areas, he is referred to works that can be found in any complete library. Refer in particular to works by Piaget, Gesell, Ilg, Flavel, Ames, Getman, Cratty, Kamii, Erikson, and Kephart, to name but a few (see Bibliography).

THE PHYSICAL EDUCATION PROGRAM: HOW IT AIDS IN PERCEPTUAL-MOTOR LEARNING AND COGNITIVE DEVELOPMENT

The following activities will serve to exemplify physical education's contribution to development in thinking processes.

Spatial Awareness

1. Who can run to the nearest wall without bumping into anyone (see chapter 3)?
2. *Freeze* (see chapter 7).
3. Who can move in a small area without touching another (see chapter 3)?
4. *Shadow* (see chapter 7).
5. Be planes at an airport at take-off without collisions (see chapter 3).
6. *Robot* (see chapter 7).

Time Concepts

1. Act out what you did at play yesterday (see chapter 3).
2. Pretend that it is lunchtime and fix a meal. When is lunchtime, before or after breakfast (see chapter 3)?
3. *What Time Is It, Mr. Fox* (see chapter 7)?

Color Concepts

1. Use a ladder: climb the green step (see chapter 6).
2. *Man From Mars* (see chapter 7).
3. *Color Tag* (see chapter 7).

Perceptual Skills

1. I say stoop, I say stand (see chapter 7).
2. *Huckle, Buckle, Bean Stalk* (see chapter 7). This game also promotes spatial awareness.
3. *Simon Says* (see chapter 7).

Motor Activities

1. Movement exploration (see chapter 3).
2. *Follow The Leader* (see chapter 7).
3. *Back-To-Back* (see chapter 7).

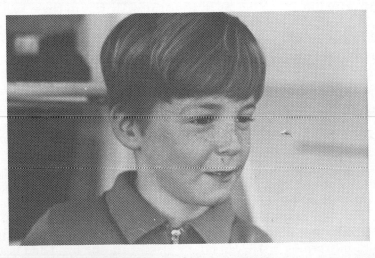

Figure 1.

Cognitive Skills

1. Sort out a bag of marbles. Which are heavy? Which are light? Is there a difference between the "cat's eye" and "puries?" When they hit each other do they all roll the same way and the same distance?
2. Have the class create its own "maze" system (see chapter 6).
3. Movement exploration: Create the letter *y* in as many different ways as you can (using all or part of the body; on different levels; with a partner and alone. See chapter 3).

THE PHYSICAL AND SOCIAL CHARACTERISTICS OF THE YOUNG CHILD; RELATED PHYSICAL EDUCATION PROGRAMS

It should be noted by the reader that *Me and I'm Great* gives *specific* details concerning children ages two through five as there is little available for teachers in this area. *General* characteristics and activities are described for children ages six through eight. Many of the games, exercises, stunts, and relay races can be expanded and adapted for older children (those from six to eight). Throughout the text, age levels are given for each activity. These are recommended ages for the *introduction* of specific skills based on a child's psychological and physiological maturity but by no means confine the activities to these specific ages. To illustrate, let us look at the game Duck, Duck, Goose (chapter 7). It can be played with as much enthusiasm by children four years of age as by those seven years of age.

Physical Characteristics Of The Two-Year-Old

At two years, a child has added 75 percent of his birth length to his height.[2] The legs grow faster than the arms, the arms faster than the trunk, and the trunk faster than the head.[3] At this stage the child generally shows a preference for the right hand, even though some do use the left and even fewer seem to have little preference.[4]

The two-year-old can build a tower of six or seven blocks. He can turn book pages easily and puts a spoon in his mouth without turning it. He can hold a glass with one hand and is able to put on a simple garment. The two-year-old's locomotor development is also more stabilized. He is able to run well and can walk up and down stairs alone. He is capable of kicking a large ball and can jump twelve inches in length.[5] Catching a ball is still a difficult task as he has not yet mastered visual processing. He leaps with one foot in front of the other and hops awkwardly.[6]

Social Characteristics Of The Two-Year-Old

The two-year-old is totally ambivalent in his feelings toward everyone and everything. He is rigid and inflexible, yet unsure of the decisions he makes. Whining and crying are constant. It is a period of frustration not only for the child but for the parent as well. Anyone familiar with the behavior of the two-year-old truly knows the meaning of the "terrible twos."

This writer can now look back with amusement and remember when her own children seemed to have a deaf ear for anyone in authority. A recording consisting of "No, don't do that; stay away from the plugs; don't punch your brother; and don't go near the street" was seriously contemplated. The two-year-old is domineering and demanding, meeting life head on. Decision making is his "thing," and takes first priority.

Two-year-olds watch others, cooperate momentarily, and often engage in the same activity as someone else, for instance shoveling or sliding, but play in an essentially solitary style. This is known as *parallel play*. However, even though they may not appear to be interacting, they seem to find a satisfaction in just being near each other.[7]

They tend to be rough with each other, hitting, and pushing, unaware of how it affects another. They recognize each other as people but are in the process of discovering characteristics in other children similar to their own. Everything is egocentric; they seek information that will eventually help them to grow beyond egocentrism.[8]

Physical Education Program

Basic skills such as walking, running, and jumping should be taught in the physical education program. Simple climbing objects should be provided that will encourage coordination and balance. Brightly-colored large balls should be utilized to give the children an opportunity to develop eye-hand coordination through two-handed bouncing and catching skills. Catching a ball is a difficult task. Most two-year-olds will keep their arms stiff rather than flexing them.

Physical Characteristics Of The Three-Year-Old

Three is a delightful age. The child of this age is "not as knowing as four but he is transcending the infantilism of two."[9] The child is now growing at a relatively slow rate compared to the rate in infancy. The average weight gain is four to five pounds. The annual growth rate is two to three inches.

Most three-year-olds can build towers of nine blocks and construct bridges of three blocks. They can catch a ball with the arms straight, copy circles, and draw straight lines. It is now possible for them to unbutton clothing and put their shoes on.[10]

Three-year-olds can balance briefly on one foot and are able to walk upstairs alternating the feet. Most have developed enough muscular strength and coordination to be able to ride a tricycle. Jumping from a bottom stair may also be accomplished. Climbing is natural and easy since the three-year-old can grip well with his hands.[11] Ladders, swings, and jungle gyms should be provided to develop skills.

Social Characteristics Of The Three-Year-Old

By the age of three, social activity has expanded considerably over the previous year. Gesell states: "On a primitive and miniature level, the third year marks a kind of adolescence, a coming of age."[12]

Three-year-olds are eager to try new experiences on their own but still need the protection of parents and teachers when difficulty occurs. They have begun to cooperate to some degree, and can now take turns with others. Their play is basically still parallel, although some do take an interest in playing together.

Children of this age are developing a desire to please and are very concerned with gaining approval for their actions. The instructor and parent must handle them with care, patience, and love. Teaching a child self-confidence during this period is essential. Constant encouragement is necessary if the child is to evolve with a good self-image. Fears of heights and of falling are common, and are often learned from fearful adults. Such fears are conditioned, and may be overcome by reconditioning or by

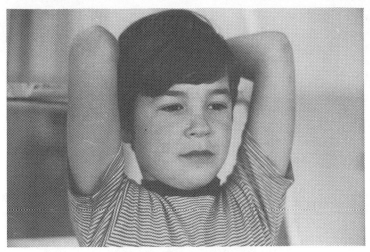

Figure 2. (Refer to page 11.)

such favorable experiences as growth in power, development of new skills, general confidence, or play therapy.[13] Tensional outlets such a blinking the eyes, sucking the thumb, and biting the nails are shown by the three-year-old. Crying and whining are triggered by the smallest of incidents, and "Do you love me?" is the question foremost in the child's mind.

Since the child possesses a vivid imagination, nightmares are common. Many children have make-believe friends whom they can actually see and hear. It is common for them to ask for two cookies, one for themselves and one for their "buddy."

They are very curious and greatly attracted to objects that are new and strange. There is much experimentation with toys and other objects in their surroundings: What do they feel like; do they come apart?

Physical Education Program

The three-year-old is a great imitator. Through imagination he learns to solve many problems. In a physical education program, many opportunities such as singing games, imitation of movements, and stories to be acted out should be provided to allow him to explore movement and stimulate his imagination. Bouncing activities should be included in the program to develop eye-hand coordination. To aid in the development of basic skills that are a prerequisite to more advanced motor skills, opportunities must be provided for climbing, pulling, and pushing objects.

Physical Characteristics Of The Four-Year-Old

The four-year-old's growth rate is similar to that of the three-year-old's. By the time children are four they have doubled their length at birth and have obtained almost one third of the weight they will have at the age of eighteen.[14]

They are now capable of cutting on a line with scissors, and can make designs and crude letters. Most children of this age can dress themselves.[15]

Leg muscles are more fully developed, and coordination has considerably improved, which enables the four-year-old to run better than the child of three. Balance has progressed to the point where walking on a beam can be done with relative ease.

The four-year-old child has a more fully developed sense of body and of spatial awareness. He can run smoothly at different

Figure 3.

speeds, turning sharply and stopping and starting quickly. Galloping can be achieved, as can descent from small ladders and short steps using alternating feet without support.[16] Catching a ball is accomplished at this stage by bending the elbows and gripping with the hands.

Social Characteristics Of The Four-Year-Old

Play for the four-year-old tends to be in small groups of two or three. Sharing does take place, although not consistently.

By this age, youngsters are aware of the opinions and attitudes of other people. They have difficulty making distinctions between truth and fiction, a natural process of development in four-year-olds. Their imagination is keenly developed and their curiosity is insatiable. Unless the parent or instructor knows the child well, she might actually believe that George, down the street, was bitten by a cobra!

Unreasonable fears, such as the fear of the dark exhibited by the three-year-old, are slowly being overcome as children progress toward the fifth year.

Physical Education Program

The program for four-year-olds should include much exploration such as role playing activities and stories to act out. They are able to participate in simple, low-organization games. Experiences in pulling, pushing, crawling over and under objects, balancing, and climbing should be included in the program to provide the widest possible experience in motor movement.

Physical Characteristics Of The Five-Year-Old

The growth of the five-year-old is relatively slow. Gain in height is greater than gain in weight. Characteristics of the middle childhood figure, the arms and legs begin to slenderize; Elkind states that "the five-year-old shows in many ways the completion of the early childhood period. Small and large muscle control and coordination are quite advanced, and independence training, clothing, eating, and toileting are about complete."[17]

The five-year-old can copy designs, letters, and numbers, and is capable of folding paper into double triangles. Since his finger-dexterity is becoming more finely developed and his mental concentration is greater, he can now tie his shoelaces and fasten buttons that he can see.[18]

The youngster of five can skip, hop on one foot ten or more times, and descend large ladders alternating the feet with ease. Walking on a straight line poses little problem. Small balls can be caught while the elbows are at the side of the body.

Social Characteristics Of The Five-Year-Old

The five-year-old seems to find himself. He has more self-motivation and can sort out the real from the make-believe. He is better able to control his frustrations and loves long, involved discussions about anything. The five-year-old is stable and fairly reliable. His mother is the center of his world. This writer found that this is where she started *liking* as well as *loving* her children. They have definite personalities that can be dealt with on a more mature level. The questions a child asks are interesting, and, although at times tiresome, essential in the development of the mental processes. The child of five displays much common sense. He works with puzzles, is fascinated by machines, and builds intricate designs with much enthusiasm and dedication.

Many youngsters start nursery school or kindergarten during this period. For a large number, it is the first experience away from the home without a parent. They must follow directions from someone new, and attempt to learn the art of self-discipline. Sharing with others is essential since they are no longer in the limelight.

The child of five is curious about everything, and the parent or teacher's role is of extreme importance. With proper stimulation the child can develop into a fascinating youngster. Simple decision making presents far less of a problem than with three- and four-year-old children. He is better able to cope with stumbling blocks, either working around them or dealing directly with them.

Physical Education Program

Incorporated into the program can be simple rhythms, swinging bats, and rope jumping. Jungle gyms provide a good opportunity for the youngster to develop his motor abilities through strength, balance, flexibility, agility, and coordination.

Movement exploration activities can be more complex and can involve mechanical items (see chapter 3) because the child's sense of spatial awareness is now well developed. Activities that allow for problem solving should be encouraged. Games as well as simplified relay races may be incorporated into the program.

Primary School Children (Six- To Eight-Year-Olds)

Generally speaking, this a period of relatively slow and constant growth. Children gradually lose their baby fat and show proportional gains in muscular tissue. This in turn gives rise to a general increase in strength, specifically in the arms and legs. Primary school age children fatigue less easily than the four- or five-year-old. When fatigue does take place, recovery is rapid after a short rest period. Hand-eye movements and reaction time are slowly improving. Coordination of small muscles becomes evident, and there is growing interest in games requiring this type of skill.

Children from ages six through eight exhibit incredible curiosity. First-graders are intrigued with number and letter concepts and delight in using these new skills. Physically, they are boisterous and fidgety. Second-graders tend to be more cautious in their approach to activities. Their actions are more self-directed and less impulsive; opportunities to act independently are welcomed. Seven-year-olds' curiosity is insatiable. They want to know the how and why of all that meets the eye. The adaptation of problem-solving activities positively reinforces their inquisitiveness. Eight-year-olds are becoming more sophisticated. Their thirst for knowledge has expanded to how, who, when, and where. Activities that utilize previously learned skills such as catching, kicking, batting, and rope climbing are recommended.

The primary school age child is in the age of conflict; his mood swings are quite dramatic. One moment he is argumentative and self assertive, and then, without warning or reason, he is cooperative and sweet. Even though parental approval is still of primary concern, "gang life" is gaining in importance.

Physical Education Program

Games requiring teams and cooperation should be included in the physical education program as well as individual skills. Children of this age need activities with a high spirit of adventure. Problem-solving skills and creativity should be encouraged.

The program should be active, incorporating the large muscles whenever possible. Games such as Kickball, Steal the Bacon, and Dodgeball are suggested. Movement experiences that emphasize perceptual-motor skills (right and left, unilateral, bilateral, and cross lateral) are of primary importance. (Refer to studies by Kephart and Delacato for further information on perceptual-motor competency.) The physical education program should be informative and instructive as well as challenging, exciting, and fun!

THE PHYSICAL EDUCATION PROGRAM: ITS ADVANTAGES IN PREPARING CHILDREN FOR SCHOOL

Parents and educators may question the necessity of a young child's physical education program, but its advantages in preparing a child for school are numerous. The following discussion will serve as a review of the major points discussed previously.

Separation From Parents

The physical education program will most probably represent the initial formal experience of separation of the child from the parent figure. This is a delicate matter and must be handled with care (see chapter 2).

Figure 4.

Socialization

The gym program will aid in the socialization of a youngster. He will learn the art of sharing both equipment and attention, and will be able to observe and learn from his peers. Initially, the child's play will be parallel in nature, but gradually he will participate with others. Social play becomes more complex as a child learns ways of approaching and interacting with others and as he develops in motor coordination, language, concepts, and imagination. Interchange increases for longer periods of time with cooperation and less conflict. The child will become more choosey with age, and expression of personal opinions will slowly creep into his behavior.

Stimulation Of The Imagination

The youngster's imagination will be stimulated through exposure to new and exciting games, apparatus, music, dramatic play, and activities in movement exploration. These are only a few of the elements that can be included in the physical education program. Creativity is encouraged, both in thinking and in movements.

Opportunity And Exposure

The physical education program gives the child an opportunity to explore many new areas. Without this chance, he may not develop discernment; how will he know if one toy is better than another for building purposes if he has but one?

He will also be exposed to a myriad of activities. This process goes hand in hand with opportunity. Without opportunity and exposure, a child remains stagnant. For example, a youngster kept in one room will never know that there is an entire world outside to be investigated.

Social Standards

The child will experience approval and disapproval of his actions from someone other than his parents or relatives. These reactions will be transmitted by the instructor and by the child's peers through gestures, facial expressions, and verbal comments.

Development Of Motor Skills

The child's motor skills will be enhanced and encouraged. A playroom filled with an assortment of items including beams, ladders, stegels, mats, balls, cones, and dumbbells will give the child the opportunity to develop balance, coordination, agility, flexibility, and strength through a guided and structured program. A well thought out plan will also leave room for freedom and spontaneous play.

Development of Thought Processes: Perceptual-Motor Learning

The physical education program will enhance thought processes. Problem solving should be encouraged in many activities. To illustrate, ask a child to determine how far he can jump from a standing position. Through personal demonstration, he answers the question (solves the problem) for himself and for the instructor as well.

The development of perceptual-motor learning is an integral part of the program. Concepts can be incorporated in the physical education program in a number of ways: through games such as *Man From Mars* (color concepts), *What Time Is It, Mr. Fox?* (concept of time), or *Freeze* and *Robot* (spatial awareness); through movement exploration such as spinning like a top without bumping into another top (spatial awareness) or painting an imaginary picture of your bedroom (color concepts); through exercises of classifying or grouping objects or events by similarities (concept of classes); through the use of apparatus such as a ladder with different-colored steps (color concept); or a rope for swinging (spatial awareness).

There are many other methods and approaches to utilize in aiding the development of thought processes. The examples cited illustrate but a few of the techniques discussed in this text. How they are best handled is left to the discretion of each instructor based on her class's needs, ability level, interests, and the instructor's own personality.

Development of Language Skills

The program facilitates the development of language skills. The child's vocabulary will be increased through terms utilized in the program (*forward, backward, line up, find a partner,* etc.). His communication powers are strengthened through comprehension (thought process) as is his ability to state what he means. By following verbal directions, he will learn organization, procedures, and use of equipment for every individual activity.

Sense Of Autonomy

A child's sense of autonomy is reinforced through the program, assuming of course that the home situation is the foundation for it. K. H. Read describes the sense of autonomy in the following way: "The teacher appreciates what it means to young children to be independent successfully, to make decisions that turn out well and to feel worthwhile in what they do. She makes the limits clear and sticks to them firmly, giving freedom within that limit. The teacher understands that the children will often test the limits she sets, as part of growing up. Because he likes her and wants to be like her, he often wants to do what he perceives the teacher wants. Thus discipline is carefully planned and carried out in such a way that children can grow in autonomy through successful deciding and doing."[19]

Development Of Interests And Preferences

The young child will learn to develop varied interests through a physical education program. He will eventually show preferences in activities. It is my opinion that all the children must participate in each activity but when given free time for play, they can choose the area they prefer. Again, this goes back to the discussion on exposure.

It is G. N. Getman's opinion that "In preparing a program of guidance for children, the development of their potential skills, parents should give particular attention to five major areas of activities:

1. General movement-patterning for the development of exploratory skills;
2. Specific movement-patterning for the development of manipulative skills;
3. Eye movement-patterning for the development of visual inspection skills;
4. Visual language-patterning for the development of communication skills;

5. Visualization-patterning for the development of interpretation skills.''

He continues by saying that "The total development of a child is the result of an interweaving of all these areas and one area affects and brings responses in all other areas through integrative development."[20]

A well designed program of physical education can have a beneficial effect upon certain children with learning disabilities as well as upon the so-called normal child. For example, data suggest that (1) movement will aid intelligence to the extent that the child is encouraged to think about the movements in which he is engaged;[21] (2) certain movement activities may aid in the improvement of specific perceptual traits, although one must be certain to teach for the transfer from motor to perceptual traits;[22] and (3) training in rhythmic perception may contribute to early success in reading.[23]

The foregoing statements are based on hypothesis, not facts. They are interesting ideas to ponder, and one wonders if, indeed, some of these are accurate. Future studies may very well indicate the correlation between the physical and cognitive skills.

As one can readily see, the physical education program offers a tremendous amount, ranging from socialization to the development of motor coordination, for the young child. It should not be assumed that he is unable to gain this experience elsewhere, but that at least in the physical education program most of the facets of thought and motor processes are joined together into one full, exciting, and beneficial program.

Notes to Chapter 1

1. Susan D. Block, "The Preschool Physical Education Program: Its Importance and Aims," *The Bulletin, Connecticut Journal of Health, Physical Education and Recreation* 22, 1(1975).
2. M. E. Breckenridge and M. N. Murphy, *Growth and Development of the Young Child*, 8th ed. (Philadelphia: W. B. Saunders, 1969).
3. Elizabeth Halsey and Lorena Porter, *Physical Education for Children* (New York: Holt, Rinehart & Winston, 1963).
4. Mollie S. Smart and Russell C. Smart, *Children, Development, and Relationships*, rev. ed. (New York: Macmillan, 1972).
5. Ibid.

 6. Halsey and Porter, *Physical Education for Children.*
 7. Smart and Smart, *Children, Development, and Relationships.*
 8. Ibid.
 9. Arnold Gesell, *The First Five Years of Life* (New York: Harper and Brothers, 1940).
10. Smart and Smart, *Children, Development, and Relationships.*
11. Halsey and Porter, *Physical Education for Children.*
12. Gesell, *The First Five Years of Life.*
13. Halsey and Porter, *Physical Education for Children.*
14. Hollis F. Fait, *Physical Education for the Elementary School Child* (Philadelphia: W. B. Saunders, 1971).
15. Smart and Smart, *Children, Development, and Relationships.*
16. Ibid.
17. David Elkind, *A Sympathetic Understanding of the Child: Birth to Sixteen* (Boston: Allyn and Bacon, 1974).
18. Smart and Smart, *Children, Development, and Relationships.*
19. K. H. Read, *The Nursery School,* 4th ed. (Philadelphia: W. B. Saunders, 1966).
20. G. N. Getman, *How to Develop Your Child's Intelligence* (Penna: Research Publications, 1962).
21. Bryant J. Cratty and Sister Margaret Mary Martin, *Perceptual-Motor Efficiency in Children: The Measurement and Improvement of Movement Attributes* (Philadelphia: Lea and Febiger, 1969). Also J. H. Humphrey, "Comparison of the Use of Active Games and Language Workbook Exercises as Learning Media in the Development of Language Understanding with Third Grade Children," *Perceptual Motor Skills* 21(1965).
22. S. D. Hill, A. H. McCullum, and A. Scean, "Relation of Training in Motor Activity to the Development of Left-Right Directionality in Mentally Retarded Children: Exploratory Study," *Perceptual Motor Skills* 24(1967).
23. P. A. Katz and M. Deutsch, "Modality of Stimulation Presentation in Serial Learning for Retarded and Normal Readers," *Perceptual Motor Skills* 19(1964). Also G. M. Sterritt and M. Rudnick, "Auditory and Visual Rhythm Perception in Relation to Reading Ability in 4th Grade Boys," *Perceptual Motor Skills* 22(1966).

Chapter 2 Effective Teaching

THE YOUNG CHILD'S PHYSICAL EDUCATION PROGRAM: ITS PURPOSE AND CONSIDERATIONS

The young child's physical education program should be an integral part of his early life experience. As previously mentioned, the program will represent his first opportunity when separated from the parent figure. He will develop relationships with peers, and learn that the world doesn't revolve around him exclusively. The preschool youngster will learn the concept of relating to a teacher rather than to his parents or relatives.

In order to make this initial experience exciting, positive, and educational, the program should be composed of many factors. Five principles well worth listing for promoting interest-development in childhood are identified by Professor John E. Anderson:

1. Bring the child to see his experiences in a different light by reorganizing his point of view.
2. Develop specific skills that enable the child to master particular demands.
3. Attach pleasant outcomes, through secondary devices (verbal and otherwise), to various activities (complimenting, building up self-esteem, encouragement).

4. Give the child good models of behavior by showing interest and enthusiasm for activities.
5. Watch particularly the incidental, casual, and indirect evaluations which, though almost automatic, may have great effects on the behavior of children.[1] (Don't be negative by saying, "That's too hard for you"; say instead, "You're terrific; I know you can do it.")

Other factors should be included in the physical education program:

1. Give the child an opportunity to explore many areas. Evidence suggests that although developing abilities will effect developing play interest, the opportunities and stimulation characterizing the child's environment will, in turn, determine the degree to which these abilities receive nurture.[2] In early years, play is life.
2. Have the experience encourage socialization. Social participation with a child's peers increases in versatility and complexity as he matures. Two-year-olds tend to be egocentric, and, during the preschool period, socialized responses increase. There is a transition from egocentricity to increased socialization (in the sense of increased cooperation).[3] Relating this to the physical education program, we find that apparatus work and movement exploration tend to be individual activities. On the other hand, games and songs move into a more sophisticated and complex level of socialization in which the concepts of sharing and cooperation are incorporated.
3. Make the class a happy experience. The instructor's main objective should be to leave the child wanting to return. This can happen if the program is exciting and positive.
4. Explore many areas in physical education. All of the following should be included: Games, songs and rhythms, stunts, apparatus work, movement exploration, free play, and exercises.
5. Take into consideration the child's socio-economic background. Try to relate to his world. Use ideas that he can understand.
6. Stimulate his imagination through fantasy, dramatic play, and music (see chapters 3 and 4).

To summarize: If the instructor makes the physical education program a rewarding, enriching, and positive experience, she cannot fail in achieving her final goal—happiness for all.

The Teacher's Role In Relating To The Young Child

There is a special breed of individual needed to work with young children. He or she must be a keen and quick observer of children's reactions and should study the behavior and potentialities of her students. Of course, the standards of ability vary from class to class and modifications should be made according to each situation.[4] One needs more than a degree in physical education or elementary education to qualify. Much of the program content is not taught in a text book. Relating to the young child takes tremendous insight and knowledge of human nature. How does one give a youngster incentive? How will one motivate his curiosity? How does the instructor know that she should leave one child alone or that another needs to be pushed? These are just a few of the questions that must be answered if the teacher is to be competent.

The following section presents a helpful set of rules serving as a guide to the instructor or parent undertaking this difficult yet very rewarding task.

1. Get to know each child at the beginning of each new session.
2. Learn his or her name and have name tags for the youngsters. There is nothing nicer than to be personally identified at the first session.
3. Start the first class with informal discussion—what is his favorite toy? What does he like to play?—followed by

Figure 5.

movement exploration. This allows the child to be himself as you (the instructor) are being yourself.

4. Be empathetic in the initial lessons, remembering that it may be the child's first experience away from his mother. The sooner rapport is established between the child and teacher, the quicker the instructor will be able to do her job. The longer the child is allowed to hang onto his mother for security, the more difficult it will be for the class as well as the teacher.

5. Encourage each child to understand that he is competing with *himself*. Young children have little knowledge of formal competition. Their only experience may be one child getting more praise than another for better performance, or sibling rivalry (see chapter 9 for a complete discussion of jealousy and competition). A child/person can be only as good in something as his physical capacity and desires permit him. He cannot be the same as his friend Billy, because he is *not* Billy. He is *himself*.*

6. Introduce the child to the room and equipment that will be used. Let him feel comfortable with his new surroundings.

7. The final, and most important step is for the instructor to be *himself*. There is nothing a child can detect faster than falseness. He is very aware of the vibrations an instructor transmits. We as parents and educators are expecting and attempting to have the child develop his own personality. We must be as honest.

The Teacher's Role In Relating To The Parents

The parents are as important to the young child's classes as are the children. Without open communication between the parent and teacher, a very valuable asset is lost. The instructor sees a student once or twice a week for forty-five minutes, which is not much time to exert a tremendous amount of influence. The parents' enthusiasm for their child's program can have carry-over value in the home situation. Some helpful suggestions when dealing with parents are as follows:

Note: This need only be discussed with children four and older if the situation presents itself.

Figure 6.

1. Talk with the parents at the first session (alone). Is there something special you should know? Does the child have any specific weaknesses you should be aware of?
2. Ask the parent why she is sending her child (only applicable in a private organization such as a YMCA). What results is she expecting?
3. Tell the parent your objectives. Take her around the class and show her how the equipment is used.
4. Ask a parent to occasionally volunteer as a spotter, or aide. (A "spotter" assists children to perform a skill.) She may be able to relate the class work to the home environment. Teach her spotting techniques when using apparatus or tumbling.
5. If a child does need a parent in the room for the first few lessons, ask her to sit on the side and observe the class. Once her child is participating, suggest the parent leave unobtrusively. Most youngsters will eventually join the group because their curiosity is aroused. The instructor may suggest that they participate and, in many cases, may carry an anxious child during class or hold his hand until he establishes some sense of security. Time should be divided equally if more than one child requires special attention.

6. Suggest to the parent when she leaves the classroom that she be *firm*. If the parent is ambivalent in her feelings about the temporary separation, the child will sense it and balk! Children are extremely aware of their parents' feelings.
7. Spend time with the parents after class, getting to know them as individuals. They can be very valuable if a class has to be cancelled or if apparatus needs to be acquired. Once you have their support they will do just about anything to help you and your program.

Free And Spontaneous Play

Free and spontaneous play is not the same as movement exploration. The latter is a guided program; free play is relatively limitless. After the first classes have taken place, this writer begins each lesson with open play. Most of the apparatus and small equipment (described in chapter 6) are left in the playroom to encourage the children to explore each piece independently. This is done after the child has had some background in each item. The free time gives the youngsters an opportunity to explore, and helps to motivate their interest.

An additional suggestion is to allow the students to play while the teacher is working with individuals on specific apparatus. For instance, if the instructor is teaching Billy to walk on the sawhorses (balance beam), the rest of the class is free to participate in other activities (bouncing a ball, walking on tires) that are not dangerous and require little supervision. Trying to keep eight to ten youngsters in a line while working with one student is unnecessary. There is a time and place for children to work together, but to expect such constant discipline is asking too much.

Setup Of The Playroom

The drawing on page 25 shows a suggested plan for the gymnasium or playroom. If the home is used, the plan can be modified by using an old mattress on the floor, a number of balls, an indoor jungle gym (toy stores have these for under $10), a hanging ladder (found for under $5), and sawhorses. Most backyards can accommodate a jungle gym and swing set; much of this equipment can be purchased inexpensively at tag sales or from neighbors with older children who have outgrown the play

apparatus. If one lives near or in an apartment complex, access to a play yard with apparatus or to a school yard and park may be possible.

The plan illustrated allows for free and spontaneous play that needs only limited supervision as the child matures.

Time Allotment And Class Outline

Young children have short attention spans; therefore classes no longer than forty-five minutes are recommended. Initially the teacher will find she needs a dozen eyes and hands, and will wonder why she has only two of each, as each child is going at his own speed and on his own level. This is but one reason parents can be an invaluable aid in assisting the instructor.

Each activity will have to be carefully explained to make sure that the students understand what is expected. A simple game such as *Wonderball* is a tremendous undertaking: the students must sit in a circle (first they must understand the meaning of a circle), follow directions, pass a ball to the player next to them, learn to sing a song, and then comprehend what to do when they are out.

The following is a suggested outline for the class period. It can be modified or expanded according to class size and ability, interests, and past experiences of the students. Ideally, class size should be limited to eight pupils per instructor. There is much need for individual attention, and too large a group will not allow for this. At least three or four activities should be included in each class.

1. Have the first class help set up the gym. It is their class and their equipment; it gives them a feeling of importance and belonging. Ask the last class of the day to help put away the equipment. It teaches the children to work together and to feel responsible for some part of the program. It is amusing to observe how enthusiastically they perform their jobs, and it becomes a game if handled properly by the instructor. Frequently the children will squabble about job priorities, much to the surprise of the parents (who can't get their children to pick up toys at home).

2. *Exercises*: Include four or five exercises to develop muscles and teach direction-following and bodily awareness.

3. *Stunts*: Forward and backward rolls, *Pyramids, Angel Stand*.

4. *Ladder work*: Jumping, climbing.

5. *Beam work*: Walk across beam, pivot, squat, crawl.

6. *Walk on tires*: Walk, jump, crawl.

7. *Rope*: Hanging and swinging or use in games.

8. *Stegel*: Walking across, over, up and down.

9. *Ball handling*: Bouncing, rolling, games.

10. *Music or game*: Songs and rhythms such as *Ring around the Rosey, Farmer in the Dell,* marching skills.

11. *Movement exploration*: This may be done in any part of the program. In my own experience, movement exploration was the "appetizer" as well as "dessert." Creating movement: Be a rabbit, leap like a frog, bury a bone like a dog.

Note: numbers 2 through 10 are discussed in detail in chapters 4 through 9.

Notes to Chapter 2

1. J. E. Anderson, "The Relation of Attitude to Adjustment," *Education* 73(1952).
2. Sidney L. Pressey and Raymond G. Kuhlen, *Psychological Development through Life Span* (New York: Harper and Brothers, 1957).

3. Robert I. Watson and Henry C. Lindgren, *Psychology of the Child,* 2nd ed. (New York: John Wiley and Sons, 1973).

4. Ivy Munden, *Physical Education for Infants* (London: University of London Press Ltd., 1953).

Chapter 3

Movement Exploration

It is a natural instinct to move. Movement, which encourages a child to discover his own physical capabilities, is first seen in an infant who waves his arms, kicks his legs, and wiggles his toes. As he develops, this gradually expands into crawling and rolling. The younger preschooler (two-and-a-half to three) can do such complex items as run, jump, and walk with relative assuredness. He becomes aware of himself and his surroundings: movement exploration is taking place.

This writer employs movement exploration as a teaching technique as well as an activity in the curriculum. An instructor, through initiation of ideas, helps a child to do "his thing." Initially, the youngster responds to the teacher's suggestions. As the child grows older, the ideas will be self-generated and acted out as he imagines. The process incorporates delving into the unknown through the use of the body and the imagination.

Movement exploration uses many media: poems, stories, small equipment, apparatus, and dramatic play. Whenever there is a call for creative thought, whether it be on a jungle gym, in an empty playroom, or while marching, this teaching technique can be utilized. Movement exploration means that all children are performing at the same time, each within his own space or area. Many activities may be done individually, although on occasion partners or groups are suggested.

Enjoyment of movement is natural. Early exposure to a happy experience in this area is necessary in order to give a youngster a solid foundation of movement skills.

Problem solving methods are incorporated in movement. Dr. Hollis Fait states that "Motor exploration for the school child takes the form of solving problems in motor movement. It is directed toward:

1. Learning what movements the body is capable of and how these may be disciplined to accomplish a desired goal;
2. Encouraging the inherent love of movement, helping to create a positive attitude toward life-long participation in motor movement;
3. Developing an understanding of the relationships of emotion to movement so that it will become possible to express emotions through movement;
4. Fostering the development of coordination, agility, flexibility, speed, and strength."[1]

The problem solving method encourages freedom and allows youngsters to search for many solutions. As an illustration, ask the children to be an inflated balloon that is suddenly popped. How does each child handle this situation? Will he shrivel up and fall to the floor? Perhaps he'll spin around the room until he runs out of air. Each child will deal with the problem differently. Initially, most will mime their peers. But once they are comfortable with their surroundings, each child will take on his own individuality.

Movement may occur in a stationary position, without moving from place to place. Different levels can be added as can be seen in the next illustration. Be a giant: How high can you reach? Kneel down and look at something small; lie on the ground and take a nap; hear a noise and stand up as quickly as you can (don't forget that you're a giant and getting up might take longer).

Movement can also be accomplished by moving from place to place. An example of this might be the following sequence: Be a train just starting to turn its wheels; go faster and pick up speed; go as fast as you can but come to a quick stop because a cow is in the middle of the track.

In movement exploration a teacher or parent can discover much about each child. Is he timid? Is he in a combative stage? Does he have a fear of monsters (the unknown)? Movement exploration can have a very positive effect if properly directed, and can be used as a tool in helping the child act out anxieties, fears, joys, and frustrations.

For two years this writer taught with no apparatus, the small equipment consisting of playground balls and clothesline rope. Three-quarters of the program dealth with movement exploration, and now, even with the additional apparatus, we still allow at least fifteen minutes for the child to be a frog, to crawl like a snake, or to be whatever his imagination creates.

A most rewarding part of the program can occur if the instructor is uninhibited. To be able to relate to the child through imagination is a rare quality, almost a gift, but it can be developed. In order to handle movement exploration well, the parent or teacher must give 100 percent of herself through her reactions, ideas, and spontaneity. It's a very exciting area, and essential for letting a child be special and unique—himself.

One of the feelings expressed by many youngsters is that of combativeness, much to the chagrin of some parents. This writer feels that it is important to discuss the sociological significance of combativeness in order to enable the reader to have a better understanding of its place in a directed program. To suppress aggression in youngsters is not wise.

"Our culture seems uncertain as to how aggressive behavior should be regarded. During childhood, aggression is discouraged, yet aggressiveness carries a premium in adult society. The ambitious, hard-driving, aggressive person represents the epitome of success in the competitive, free-enterprising system. Aggressiveness appears to be approved in covert, sophisticated forms, but frowned upon in the overt, primitive, physical sorts that characterize children's behavior, except in such formalized events as athletic contests and war."[2]

If he is guided in constructive ways, the child will benefit in later life. Suppressing a basic instinct can only hurt, not aid, a child, even though the parent or teacher's intentions are well-meaning.

As adults, we are combative in a positive as well as a negative sense. We argue, have discussions, and disagree based upon our individual beliefs. But these beliefs had to start someplace, and learning to defend our ideas comes from aggressions in early childhood. In adulthood, combativeness takes on a different form, but it all comes from the same roots. It is but one small part of problem solving. We are exposed to, or create, situations that require the weighing of values in order to come to decisions. Through discussions, we learn other peoples' viewpoints and hopefully draw personal conclusions based upon a myriad of ideas. The foundation for our opinions starts in early childhood, where we learn what is and what is not acceptable in our environment. Examples of positively directed combativeness in a game situation are *Dodgeball, Cat and Dog,* or *Kickball* (see chapter 7).

In movement exploration, aggression is handled differently. The instructor may suggest that the class try to capture a ferocious lion or wrestle an ornery alligator. Through this medium the child is allowed physically to struggle with an imaginary animal, tying him up and dragging him back to the teacher for praise for a difficult job well done.

METHODOLOGY

The teacher should initially set the framework for movement in which, as previously mentioned, problem solving techniques are incorporated. A child must figure out what he must create with his body in order to get the desired results. Great care should be exercised in describing the situations, allowing for a variety of responses and offering a choice of exploration or alternatives. Limits should not stifle the children. There should be much of "Who can?" and "Let's try."

ACTIVITIES

The inclusion of *Areas Of Development* in the next section is designed to further clarify the purpose of each activity. For example, if the children create an inchworm or dinosaur with their hands and fingers it will aid in the development of dexterity.

ACTIVITIES	AREAS OF DEVELOPMENT
1. *Who can think of different ways to* :	
Spin like a top?	Balance and leg muscles.
Leap like a frog?	Explosive movement and leg muscles.
Reach way up to the sky?	Toes, legs, arms stretched.

Fold up like a flower at night?	Contraction of body; all parts are used.
Walk forward?	Leg muscles and balance.
Move in a small area without touching another?	Body and spatial awareness (coordination).
Crawl backwards?	Arm and leg muscles.
Swim like a fish?	Bent at waist, arm muscles developed.
Make a dinosaur with the fingers?	Finger dexterity-small hand muscles.
Swing legs and arms?	Arms and legs as well as balance.
Run to the nearest wall and back without bumping into anyone?	Body and spatial awareness (coordination).
Flap the arms like a bird?	Arm muscles.
Gallop like a horse?	Leg muscles.
Make a big circle with the arms?	Arm muscles.
Lift a heavy piece of imaginary wood?	This is an isotonic exercise where a child is lifting an imaginary force. If done properly, the entire body will be used starting from a crouched position to an upright one, using arms and legs.

Figure 7. Spin.

Make the letter *Y* or *A* (or any letter of the alphabet) with your fingers, hands, or whole body, alone or with a partner?

Cognitive development; flexibility, agility, spatial awareness.

Make any number from one to ten with your body?

Cognitive development, agility, flexibility, spatial awareness.

Make a triangle, square, or circle with your body?

Cognitive development, spatial awareness, problem solving, coordination.

2. *Show Me How:*

(There is spatial awareness in all *Show Me How* activities. Encourage a variety of responses.)

Figure 8. Lifting heavy wood.

Figure 9. Making the letter Y with the legs . . .

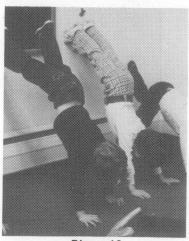

Figure 10. . . . with the whole body . . .

Figure 11.
. . . and with the arms.

Figure 12. *Making the letter X
with the arms . . .*

Figure 13.
. . . with a partner . . .

Figure 14.
. . . and with the whole body.

To kick the ball.	Leg muscles, balance.
To be a giant.	Entire body is expanded.
To bounce like a ball.	Large skeletal muscles (when moving from semi-squat to upright position).
To chug, chug and move like a train.	Arms and legs.
To make a bridge. (What kinds of bridges are there?)	Arm and leg strengthening, flexibility, cognitive skills.
To march like a soldier.	Leg muscles, proper stance.
To be an inchworm, using the fingers.	Finger dexterity, small hand muscles.
To reach for a star.	Stretching exercise.
To dive from a board.	Run, jump, bend.
To roller-skate.	Leg muscles, balance.
To ride a bicycle.	Leg muscles.

3. *Animals*

Ducks' swimming lesson.	Arms and legs.
Hopping like a bunny.	Legs.
Eating a carrot like a rabbit.	Facial muscles.
Walk and cluck like a chicken.	Arms bent at elbows, legs.
Wave the trunk like an elephant.	Arms and legs.
Fly like a butterfly.	Arms and legs.
Be a honeybee.	Running, change of direction.
Hiss and crawl like a snake.	Facial muscles (tongue going in and out), arms.
Capture a fly and jump from a lily pad like a frog.	Facial muscles (in croaking); legs (in leaping and landing).
Lap milk like a cat.	Facial muscles.
Bury a bone like a dog.	Hands and legs.
Eat a banana like a monkey.	Hand and facial muscles.
Make a nest like a bird.	Entire body, depending on how active a "bird" is in building a nest.

4. *Things* (Encourage Variety.)

Go on a ride: Train: be a conductor.	Many muscles of the body, depending upon the child's imagination

Figure 15. The train starts . . .

Figure 16. . . . and falls.

Plane: be the pilot.
Boat: be the captain.
Car: be the driver.
Bicycle: be the rider.

Go to a restaurant: order and eat dinner.

Leg, arm, and facial muscles.

Go through a toy store and act out some of the toys you choose: become a jump rope, a doll, a marble.

Can involve most muscles of the body.

Be planes at an airport (*Piper Cub, 747 jet*): do take-offs and landings; be a plane with engine trouble. (All of these should be done with no collisions.)

Body and spatial awareness (running without obstructing another's path); change of direction.

Be a fireman. Sleep, dress, go to a fire, put it out, come back to the firehouse.

All the body muscles, especially the arm and leg muscles.

Go to a zoo and feed the animals.

Leg and arm muscles.

Search for monsters. (This can be made fun and unfearful for children if handled carefully by teacher. It is important for the children to know that there are friendly monsters who are green and who eat *Crackerjacks*.)

All muscles of the body are involved, depending on the complexity of the skit.

Cut the grass with a lawnmower.

Arm and leg muscles.

Climb a tree. (What does it look like? Is it big? Frail? What happens in a wild storm?)

Arm and leg muscles.

Be a log and roll down a hill.

Balance.

Make a snowman.

Leg muscles (bending to roll snow); arm muscles (making the snowman).

Build a house.

Problem solving; many muscles are involved by imaginary lifting, carrying, loading, hammering, etc.

Bake a cake.

Hand and arm muscles.

and energy; also cognitive skills, spatial awareness.

Blow and break soap bubbles.	Facial muscles.
Be Indians. Smoke a peace pipe, send out smoke signals, sing a rain dance song, ride a horse.	Many muscles are involved, depending upon what activity is chosen.
Be a statue and hold that position. (What type will the children be: soldier, horse, bathing beauty?)	Balance; other muscles depending on what type of statue is chosen.
Walk on a tightrope.	Balance and foot muscles.
Be a piece of corn sizzling in hot fat and *pop*!	Explosive movement.
Blow up like a balloon, spinning around as they do when deflated. Try different ways of deflating. *Wind*	Cognitive skills, spatial awareness, many muscles can be used when going from small to large to small.

5. *Holidays*

Be a Fourth of July firework explosive. (Noisy, silent, or slow?)	Use of the entire body in an explosive movement.
Decorate a Christmas tree.	Arms and legs.
Light a Menorah.	Arms and hands.
Be a turkey and run away from Indians on Thanksgiving.	Vocal and large muscles (through running).
Stuff a turkey.	Arms.
Act out a Thanksgiving skit involving Pilgrims, Indians, and turkeys.	Many muscles, depending on complexity of the skit.
Have a parade for Memorial Day.	Large and small muscles. (Large skeletal muscles when marching and lifting legs for high step; small muscles, especially finger muscles, when flute-playing.)
Pass out pretend-valentines as a postman.	Arms and legs.
Be an Easter bunny.	Leg muscles (hopping).
Hide eggs and find them.	Bending and stretching, flexibility.
Halloween. What will you be: witch, ghost, scarecrow?	Many muscles can be involved depending on child's choice of character.

6. *Professions And People*

  Be a:

    Teacher.
    Housewife.
    Doctor.
    Painter.
    Veterinarian.
    Hairdresser.
    Milkman.
    Garbage Collector.
    Daddy.
    Mother.
    Grocery Store Clerk.
    Carpenter.
    Dentist.
    Salesperson.
    Artist.
    Nurse.
    Postman.
    Sailor.
    Grandfather (How does he
      walk and talk?).
    Window Washer (on a high
      building).
    Grandmother.
    Astronaut.

All *Professions And People* activities will involve large and small muscles depending on how detailed the children are with the professions. These activities also develop cognitive skills.

7. *TV And Cartoon Characters*

    Popeye
    Big Bird
    Three Bears
    Santa Claus
    Fat Albert
    Porky Pig
    Six-Million-Dollar Man
    Jack And The Beanstalk
    Three Little Pigs
    Shazam And Isis
    Pluto
    Sleeping Beauty
    Cookie Monster
    Cinderella
    Little Miss Muffet
    Tooth Fairy
    Bugs Bunny

Cognitive skills; other muscles depending on the type of character the child chooses and what he does with his imagination. Perceptual-conceptual learning; nose and facial muscles.

Fast and slow motion.

Daffy Duck
Magilla Gorilla
Mickey Mouse
Jack and Jill
Snoopy
Wonderwoman

8. *Senses*

a. *Smell*:   Cognitive skills; facial muscles.

How does it smell after it
rains on a hot day?

Bread-baking.

Something rotten.

A skunk.

b. *Touch*:   Perceptual-motor learning; feet,
                                     hands, and facial muscles.
Sticky candy.

Touch ice (how does it feel?).

Walk in sand.

Walk through mud (does it
ooze through your toes?).

Touch cotton candy (how
does it feel? What does
the tongue do?).

Touch a porcupine.

c. *Taste*:   Facial muscles.

Something sweet.

Something sour.

Something bitter.

Cotton candy (how do you
eat it?).

Spaghetti (how do you eat it
if it is very long?).

Pizza (when it is gooey and
very hot?).

Soup (when it's cold?).

d. *See And React To Or Become:*   Facial muscles and big muscles.

A big rain cloud.

A friendly giant that wants to
play.

A dog show. What kinds of dogs are there? Act them out.

A big snake in a tree.

e. *Hear And React:*

  A train coming and you are on the track.

  A car's horn.

  A big lion coming after you.

  Thunder and lightning. (Many children have a fear of thunder and a game situation can help to overcome the anxieties they feel. How do the children react to the sounds?).

Facial and leg muscles; decision making and spatial awareness.

9. *Seasons*

Perceptual-motor learning.

a. *Fall:*

  Rake leaves.

Large skeletal muscles in gross movement.

  Be a falling leaf.

Jumping, whirling, falling.

  Jump in a pile of leaves.

Small muscles.

  Be a wind storm, making noises, jumping and moving, whirling around.

Facial muscles (when making sounds).

b. *Spring:*

  Be a flower growing.

  Walk in the rain.

  Plant a garden.

  Be a worm after a rainfall.

Large skeletal muscles in gross movements (running, walking, crawling); small muscles in hand movements (planting flowers, for example).

c. *Winter:*

  Go skating, sledding.

  Build a snowfort.

  Shovel snow.

  Slip on ice.

  Jump in snow.

Large skeletal muscles for gross movements (skating, lifting, jumping); small muscles (hands and fingers) while building snow-forts.

d. *Summer:*

  Swimming.

Arms and leg muscles.

Building sand castles.	Finger dexterity.
Fishing.	Arm muscles.
Boating.	Arm muscles.
Surfboard riding.	Balance.
Finding seashells.	Flexibility.
Seeing a shark while in the water.	Facial muscles (fear); big muscles while swimming.

10. *Sports*

Act out in groups or alone:

Baseball ("Batter up").	All sports will incorporate leg and arm muscle development. They will also include development of balance, agility, flexibility, and change of level and direction.
Soccer.	
Football.	
Basketball.	
Gymnastics.	
Boating.	
Swimming.	
Golf.	
Tennis.	
Dancing.	
Archery.	

11. *Complex Ideas With And Without Partners*

Cowboys and Indians.	Leg muscles.
Sledding in snow.	Balance, leg muscles.
Bus ride to the beach: Find shells, get something to eat, make castles, and swim.	
Bear Hunt (see below).	
Take an imaginary car ride (see below).	
Be an animal and visit a "People Shop."	All muscles will be employed. Problem solving, decision making, creative thought processes.

12. *Time Concepts*

Act out what you did yesterday at play. Pretend it is lunch-	All muscles will be employed depending upon the complexity of the skit.

time. When is it? Is it after
breakfast? Fix a meal. What
will you have? Soup, a ham-
burger, spaghetti?

Dinosaurs were here before you
were born. What would you
act like if you were a big,
ferocious dinosaur? What
would you eat?

*Bear Hunt

Setup: Group may sit in a circle or in front of the instructor. Children repeat and do motions exactly like the teacher's after she has spoken.

TEACHER: Let's go on a bear hunt. (Hands alternate hitting legs as if walking.)
CHILDREN: (Repeat.)
TEACHER: OK, let's go!
CHILDREN: (Repeat.)
TEACHER: There's a tree.
CHILDREN: (Repeat.)
TEACHER: Can't go over it.
CHILDREN: (Repeat.)
TEACHER: Can't go under it.
CHILDREN: (Repeat.)
TEACHER: Have to climb up it.
CHILDREN: (Repeat.)
(Teacher puts hands around pretend tree and goes higher and higher, then comes down the tree in the same manner. Children do the same.)
TEACHER: There's a swamp.
CHILDREN: (Repeat.)
TEACHER: Can't go over it.
CHILDREN: (Repeat.)
TEACHER: Can't go under it.
CHILDREN: (Repeat.)
TEACHER: Have to walk through it.
CHILDREN: (Repeat.)
(Teacher makes a face, spreads her hands out in front of her and then pulls her hands up to signify walking with shoes that are sticking in the mud. She also makes a sloshing sound every time her hands lift up out of the mud. Children do the same.)
TEACHER: There's a river.
CHILDREN: (Repeat.)
TEACHER: Can't go over it.
CHILDREN: (Repeat.)
TEACHER: Can't go under it.
CHILDREN: (Repeat.)

TEACHER: Have to swim through it.
CHILDREN: (Repeat.)
(Teacher then swims by using arms over in a crawl stroke. Children do the same. They then make a walking sound with hands on legs.)
TEACHER: Shshh...... (Puts her finger up to lips and looks around as if hearing something. Then she yells...) It's a bear, run!!
(Children do the same as the teacher. By this point they're so excited that they're shouting with glee.)
TEACHER: Go over the river. (She is using the swimming stroke.)
CHILDREN: (Repeat.)
TEACHER: Go over the swamp. (Makes sloshing sounds and pulls hands up and down through the mud.)
CHILDREN: (Repeat.)
TEACHER: Go up the tree. (Quickly climbs up and down the tree with hands.)
CHILDREN: (Repeat.)
TEACHER: Whew! We made it! (Picks arm up and shuts pretend door and wipes her forehead out of relief. Children do the same.)

*Car Ride

Each child sits in a tire, or on a sawhorse or jungle gym. The teacher suggests visiting a place such as a zoo, toy store, or jungle. (As the children mature and become familiar with the game, they will make the suggestions). They bounce up and down making motor sounds of a car and then squeal their brakes to a fast halt. They jump out of their car and run to the other side of the playroom, bringing back imaginary animals such as lions or snakes they have captured at the teacher's suggestion. After each new capture (always bringing back their captives to the instructor), they again climb back into the car until they "see" another wild animal and the game is repeated four or five times. The younger child may not know what to do and can either follow the group, if he is more outgoing, or sit with the teacher holding onto the imaginary animals the instructor has been given to "guard."

How each child approaches this idea is an experience in itself. Some are kind to their "captives" while others are forceful and rough. In many cases it really does look as if they're wrestling with a lion.

The behavior they exhibit will be under control if you have the children return to the instructor with their animals. (Some children will have to be called back because their "car" is ready to leave on the next excursion.)

13. *Action Ideas And Dramatic Play*

Get dressed. What will you wear?	Finger dexterity, flexibility, and balance, i.e., standing on one foot while putting on slacks.
Put on Mommy's makeup.	Facial and finger development.

Climb a mountain.	Leg muscles.
Build a fire.	Arm and leg muscles.
Pitch a tent.	Arms, legs stretching, flexibility.
Clean a house.	Leg and small muscles.
Go grocery shopping.	Arms, legs, and facial development.
Pretend you're eating something and have the group guess what it is (i.e., licking an ice cream cone).	Facial muscles and arms are used depending upon choice.
Grab bag: Have children pretend to be a toy out of a grab bag (i.e., march like a toy soldier, roll up and jump up and down like a ball, lie on the back and cry like a baby).	Whole body will be used depending upon choice of toy; cognitive development.

Mechanical items:

Group of children each pretend to be a part of a machine, such as a washing machine: Child A turns around like tumbling clothes. Child B pivots back and forth like the agitator of the washer. Child C is the *on-off* button of the machine and goes up or down. Child D is the water in the machine, moving up and down and around while gurgling.	Entire body is used depending upon what part of the machine a child chooses to act out; cognitive development.

Other examples might include:

Sewing machine.

Iron.

TV set.

Mixer.

Electric coffee pot.

14. *Exploration* (using running, leaping, stopping, and change of direction).	Spatial awareness for all activities.
Run on toes as quietly as possible.	Foot muscles, leg muscles, balance.

Run, stop short, pivot and turn around, and run back.	Leg muscles.
As you run, leap as high as you can.	Leg muscle development; explosive movement.
Leap like a deer, stop and eat grass, then run as if startled.	Leg muscles.
Try a hop, tiptoe, crawl, and log roll.	Flexibility, balance, and leg muscles.
Run sideways.	Coordination and leg muscles.
Run in a zigzag around cones.	Coordination and leg muscles.
Run low, touching the ground.	Balance, leg muscles.

15. *Exploring* (with cones, balls, and other objects).

Bounce a ball with two hands.	Eye-hand coordination.
Throw a ball as high as possible.	Arm muscles, eye-hand coordination.
Throw a ball to a partner.	Eye-hand coordination.
Crawl around cones.	Arm and leg muscle development.
Jump over lines drawn on floor.	Muscle development of legs.
Run and leap over tires.	Muscle development of legs.

16. *TV Commercials*

| Popcorn machine Talking cereals Scrubbing Bubbles Bread ads—being squeezed Tablet fizzing in water | Entire body used depending upon upon activity child chooses. |

It is important to note that some of the items mentioned above are applicable only in certain geographic locations. A child living in Florida, for example, may have no conception of snow. The teacher may wish to omit discussion of winter or may include the concept of seasonal change as a learning tool. Another example might be the city child who has never built a fire or pitched a tent. These activities present a good opportunity for the adult to expose the children to situations that differ from their own.

Movement exploration should be varied according to the individual differences of each child. A younger class (ages two-and-a-half to four) will need the ideas simplified; the older ones (five and older) can carry out more complex activities involving mechanical items, dramatic plays, or sense of touch with little aid from the instructor.

Movement exploration is a marvelous technique for the parent to use on rainy days or with a bed-ridden child. The beauty of movement exploration is that it requires no equipment, little space, and develops a youngster's mind and body while being entertaining and fun.

Notes to Chapter 3

1. Hollis F. Fait, *Physical Education for the Elementary School Child* (Philadelphia: W. B. Saunders, 1971).
2. Johnson, Ronald C., and Gene R. Medinnus, *Child Psychology: Behavior and Development* (New York: John Wiley & Sons, 1967).

Chapter 4

Rhythmic Activities, Creative Movement, Singing And Musical Games

THE RHYTHMIC PROGRAM

Rhythmic movement should be part of every young child's physical education program. Children have a natural love of music. Learning to create through bodily movement is an integral part of the program. Through large-muscle movement and locomotor patterns (moving from place to place), youngsters gain a better understanding of the use of their bodies.

The young child's concepts of space, like his concepts of time, are derived from bodily experience. During the sensori-motor period, he touches, looks, mouths, and moves to build concepts of his body and of other objects.[1] Initially, everything a child does through movement and perceptions is egocentric. As he grows older, the youngster applies more order to the way in which he deals with objects in space; he becomes more organized and more oriented to his surroundings. This writer can recall her niece who, at the age of two, would hide behind a small tree and assume that no one could see her because she could not see them.

Rhythmical movements aid the youngster in relating to his surroundings. If he is galloping, he will have to turn sharply to avoid colliding with a wall or another child. He will learn the concepts of force, speed, change of direction, and change of level through movement. Eventually he will be able to listen for beat patterns or changes in musical tempo.

Rhythmical activities allow all children to participate. In the early years (two-and-a-half to four) it is done by miming peers or the instructor. As the child becomes familiar with the various beats and gains confidence in his body (because it begins to move the way he commands), he becomes more creative. As a group of California school supervisors concluded, "Rhythmic bodily movements, with or without music, becomes a medium of art expression. As in any other act, the child may make use of the medium in any of various ways according to his level of development."[2]

Movement expression through rhythm offers good opportunities for incidental and direct teaching of the workings of the body and of proper alignment. Good posture is absolutely essential. The sooner a child develops this, the more natural it will become as he matures (see chapter 3).

The rhythmical program consists of fundamental rhythms, creative movement, and singing games such as singing along with or performing to records and marching.

Many texts include folk dances, but it is this writer's opinion that they should be eliminated from a preschool program. If a child has been taught basic rhythms and simple song-games he will be well prepared for folk dances upon reaching the primary grades. Even simple folk music is far too complex for the average two-and-a-half to four-and-a-half-year-old. At six years of age he can learn one of many folk dances such as the *Mexican Hat Dance*, but before that time the many involved steps might defeat rather than encourage him.

TEACHING RHYTHMS

Basic Movements

A child should properly learn basic movements. Walking, running, and jumping are but a few of these, and for each there is what might be termed a "natural" movement. Variations and ideas should proceed from this base.

Variations:

Once basic movements have been established, variations can be incorporated. A child can perform a relevé (on tiptoes), with feet flexed (turned upward), with knees bent, kicking high in the air, and in a sitting position.

1. Change of direction: Basic movement can be varied by, for example, walking in a straight line, walking in a small circle, or cutting across the floor to make a diagonal line.
2. Change of level: Sitting, standing, lying, or kneeling.
3. Change of focus: Looking up, down, over one's shoulder, under the legs, etc.

Time Factor

Movement can be performed at different speeds and with various beats, either separately or combined. It is suggested that the child start with separate beats (i.e., one-two-three, one-two-three). Combinations should be the last of events since they are a difficult coordination task for the preschooler (i.e., one-two-three, one-two, one-two-three, one-two-three-four).

Space Patterns

A child learns the many directions he can cover with rhythms. In a room he can cut diagonally across the floor or zig-zag from one corner to another. He can imagine that he is big, small, wide, or tiny (see chapter 3).

Force

The intensity of rhythms can be conveyed through heavy, medium, or light emphasis. A child may move heavily like an elephant or walk quietly and smoothly like a panther; he may pretend to pull a heavy object or push a balloon.

BASIC MOVEMENT PATTERNS

Use of the hands by clapping and hitting a tomtom or tamborine is essential in teaching rhythms.

Walk____ ___ ___ ___ ___ ___ ___ ___ ___ ___ ___*

Run_____*

Skip____ _____ _ _____ _____ _ _____ _____ _ _____ _ _____

Gallop

Slide

*____Long clap with pause

___Short series of claps

Tiptoe_ _ _ _ _ _ _ _ _ _ _ _(half the size of a run)

Swing _____ _ _____ _ _____ _ _____

Hop _____(same as run)

Jump

Walking

The weight of the body is transferred from the heel to the ball of the foot, then to the toes for the push-off. The toes should be pointing straight ahead (watch for weakness in the arches of the feet of the children) with the body erect (not with shoulders thrown back) and the arms swinging freely from the shoulders (in opposition to the extended foot).

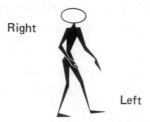

Right

Left

Running

Running starts out as a fast walk and continues until there is a period of suspension with emphasis on the spring from the toes. The body should bend slightly forward with the elbows bent, *moving rhythmically* and in opposition to the feet. Some children will do one of two things:

1. Run flat footed rather than from heel to toe with a spring.
2. Swing the same arm as the extended foot. This will cause the body to roll from side to side rather than remain erect.

Jump

Feet are together. The child pushes his weight from the heels to high toes for the spring. The arms aid in the jump with an upswing. The jump may be performed up and down in a stationary position, side to side, forward, or backward, ending with a semi-squat to stand. The novice jumper will perform this one foot at a time rather than with both feet moving simultaneously. Emphasize feet being "glued together."

Hop

The body weight is on one foot with the other leg bent at the knee and raised off the floor. Arms are bent at the elbows. There will be one major problem: balance. Until the foot arch and toes are developed, the child will have the tendency to lower the raised foot for stability as he moves forward, up and down, or side to side.

Gallop

The child should face forward with the left foot extended on the floor, lifting the right foot to meet the left, following directions to *step left—together right—step left—together right;* increase the tempo. The class should learn to gallop starting with either foot.

Note: The instructor should face the students and ask them to repeat her movements (mirror-image) in the *Gallop* and *Slide*, since most preschoolers do not know right from left.

Slide (A gallop to the side)

The child stands facing the teacher and extends the left foot to the side, lifting the right foot to meet the left and repeating the process: *step left—together right—step left—together*; slowly increase the tempo. The slide can be performed starting with either foot.

Skip

The *Skip* is the most difficult rhythm for the younger child to perform and should be taught last. It is a series of step-hops done with alternate feet. Ask the students to take a step with one foot followed by a small hop on the same foot. Then they take a step with the other foot and a hop on that foot. The arms swing freely and in opposition to the feet.

Indian Step

This is a variation of the *Skip* and fun for toddlers as they may add war whoops. It is performed by doing two hops on the right foot and two on the left. The step may be done in any number of ways: side to side; forward; backward. Use of the hands may be added for creativity as in the *Indian Rain Dance*.

Leaping

The *Leap* is an elongated running step with the legs spread widely apart and is designed to cover distance or to go over low obstacles. It may be combined with small runs, i.e., *run, run,*

Figure 17. . . . The Indian Step . . .   *Figure 18. . . . and with a hop.*

leap, run, run, leap. Only the older children (four to five years) can be expected to perform the *Leap.*

MOVEMENT EXPLORATIONS AND RHYTHMS

Utilize movement exploration with rhythms. Create a story incorporating the various beat patterns after the basic movements have been taught. It may be handled as described below. The teacher asks the children to act out any work that shows movement, i.e., *walk, tiptoe, run.*

The hunter *walks* softly through the woods. He hears an animal and *tiptoes* slowly in a crouched position. Stopping to take aim with his gun, he realizes the wild tiger is charging him and *runs* as fast as possible diagonally across the floor.

Additional Suggestions:

1. Walk:—tall like a giant,
    heavy like an elephant,
    slow like an old man,
    tiptoe like Tinker Bell,
    bent over like an elephant.
  Hop, slide, jump: like a rabbit, kangaroo, frog.
  Gallop: like a horse or deer.
  (Combine any two.)
2. Utilizing space: move forward, backward, side, diagonal, circle, small, big, crawl, kneel, lie down, roll.
3. Imitating for a story:
    a. Pets—cat (curls up, stretches, arches back, sits up, jumps).
    b. Zoo—monkey, birds, snakes.
    c. Wind-up toys—doll, soldier, monkey.

CREATIVITY IN RHYTHMS USING BALLS, ROPES, DUMBBELLS, AND MARCHING

Ball Skills

1. Bounce and catch. Vary the number of bounces.
2. Dribble a ball.

3. Crawl and push the ball with the head across the floor.
4. Throw a ball against a wall and catch it (an advance skill).
5. Pass a ball around a circle from child to child or with partners.
6. Toss the ball into the air: how high can it go?

Rope-Jumping Skills

1. Swing rope back and forth.
2. Change speed of rope swing, i.e., *very s-l-o-w, medium slow, fast*.
3. Eventually work up to turning the rope in a circle. Most children will not be able to do this until the age of five or six since it takes a tremendous amount of eye-foot coordination.
4. Pretend rope is a snake or worm and wiggle it.

Dumbbells

1. Ask the children to make moving circles with their arms while holding the dumbbells. At the same time have them walk forward, march, or run. This task is much harder to perform than it appears. The youngsters must do one step automatically while thinking about the other. (This is similar to patting the head while rubbing the tummy.)
2. Raise and lower the dumbbells from a standing, to kneeling, to lying position in continuous movement. This is an excellent test for body balance as the children won't be able to use their hands on the floor when changing positions.

Marching

Marching is a multi-faceted area that develops muscle coordination through rhythms, direction-following, discipline, and group participation. Marching music varies from slow to fast, from solemn to gay. It may be handled from simple (one line moving forward), to complex (various group patterns either in opposition or as a unit).

Small equipment may be incorporated. Children can use dumbbells or balls, walk over tires, or walk around cones and tom-toms to create more complex and interesting marching

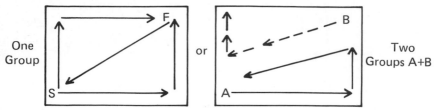

patterns. The youngsters can also become various characters: baton twirler, clown, soldier, bathing beauty, or cowboy on a horse. All of the suggestions may be utilized but it is important to remember that the marching step (a high leg lift with a bent knee) must still continue throughout the activity.

When first attempting to teach the preschooler marching techniques, you may find the following suggestions helpful:

1. Line up children with the more advanced student at the head and the teacher at the end (so she can see all the students).
2. Start with a simple marching step in place and practice going around the room, walking in straight lines and turning sharply when reaching the corners.
3. Put the exercise to music.
4. Make sure the students follow the person directly in front of them. The teacher may hold the hands of one or two children when first attempting the march. As they become familiar with the activity most will stay in line.
5. Add commands after the youngsters are acquainted with marching:
   a. *Forward march; halt; about face.*
   b. *Freeze; turn; stop.*
   c. *Green (go); red (stop); pivot (turn).*
6. *About face* or *pivot* are essential commands that allow each child the opportunity to be the leader. Have the old leader exchange places with the new one to avoid confusion over their positions.
7. Add variety of floor patterns. If the group is advanced and at least five years of age, ask the children to work in two groups performing opposite floor patterns. Have a parent be in one group while the instructor is with the other.
8. Add the use of supplies and characters while marching.
9. Create a maze system using cones, ropes, and tires in various places around the playroom. Walk through what is expected before putting the march to music. It should be

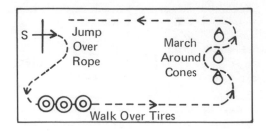

noted that teaching marching is no simple task. Youngsters' attention spans are extremely short. Keeping children in straight lines is almost impossible—therefore by shortening the length of the line the problems can be lessened. Keep the activity short, sweet, and at a fast pace.

REVIEW

Fundamentals

1. March in procession.
2. March on lines drawn or taped on the floor. (If there aren't any lines you can make them with masking tape.)

Suggested Variations

(Still utilizing the same marching beat):
1. Change of level: walk, kneeling, crawling.
2. Change of direction: diagonal, circle.
3. Change of number: three march to one corner while three march to other corner and both come back together to be in straight line.
4. Variety of movement: march on tiptoe with knees bent.
5. Add use of supplies: tom-toms, dumbbells.
6. Add use of equipment: tires, cones, ropes.

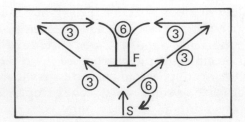

S = Start

F = Finish

Movement Exploration

Ideas that teachers may use to add variety to the activity:
1. Animal parade: each child is a different animal from a zoo.
2. Western parade: cowboys, Indians, bucking broncos, Indian princesses.
3. Toy parade: dolls, soldiers.
4. Holiday parade: flag carriers, drummers, fife players, baton twirlers, old cars (honk, sputter), fire engines.

ACTIVITY SONGS AND POEMS

The following criteria should be considered when choosing activities, songs, and poems:
1. Is there movement throughout the chosen piece? Will the children be motivated by it?
2. Is the content within the children's experience? Don't forget their young age.
3. Is the main idea suitable for their age level, ability, and comprehension?
4. Will the children enjoy the composition?[3]

Figure 19. Parade on tires.

Poems For Movement

There are many suitable poems such as Robert Louis Stevenson's "I Have a Little Shadow," that can be done by miming a partner. A resourceful and creative teacher can write her own verses. Have the children act out words that are descriptive. The teacher may emphasize these words by her tone.

Balloon

I'm a bright red *balloon* that is *little* and *flat*,
I'm being *blown* up, what do you think of that?
Away I will *fly*,
Up to the *sky*,
Pop—now I'm *small*,
It was fun being *tall*!

Weather

Swish goes the wind,
It makes the leaves *fly*.
Whoops, there's *thunder*
and *lightning* up *high*.
Down comes the *rain*
In buckets so *big*.
In a near farm it's just cleaned a *pig*.
Out comes the *sun*, so yellow and bright,
It's drying the wetness with all of its might.

Songs

Ring Around The Rosey

Age Level: Two years and older.
Purposes: Direction-following and holding onto partner's hands while moving at the same time.
Organization: Circle formation holding hands.
Verses: Ring around the rosey,
          Pocket full of posey,
          Ashes, ashes (children circle clockwise),
          All fall down! (Break apart and fall down.)
Repeat.
Things to watch for: Children will have the tendency to pull apart while in circle and try to "fall down" before ending. Tell them to drop hands and fall (not pull partners with them).

Note: This is also an excellent game to play in shallow water if children have a fear of getting their faces and bodies wet.

London Bridges

Record: Put out by many companies or song may be sung by class.

Age Level: Two-and-a-half years and older.

Purpose: Direction-following; learning to be a good sport if captured; learning to take turns being a bridge (which they will all want).

Organization: Single circle moving clockwise. Two children are chosen to form a bridge by facing each other, joining hands high in the air. Children go under "bridge" all built up.

Verses: London Bridge is all built up, all built up, all built up,
London Bridge is all built up,
My fair lady.

London Bridge is half built up, half built up, half built up,
London Bridge is half built up,
My fair lady. (Children forming bridge drop one hand, leaving only half of the bridge.)

London Bridge is falling down, falling down, falling down,
London Bridge is falling down,
My fair lady. (Hands slowly come down on "my fair lady." Bridge captures child walking under bridge by joining hands on either side of "lady.")

Take a key and lock her up, lock her up, lock her up. (Repeat.)

My fair lady. (Moves back and forth gently rocking captured lady in "jail.")

(Repeat song with new bridge. One side is "captured lady.")

Things to watch for: Keep the children in a walking formation without "cutting" in line. Emphasize not being rough when capturing the "lady."

I'm A Little Teapot

Age Level: Two-and-a-half years and older.
Purpose: Fun and direction-following.
Organization: Stand in circle formation.

Verses: I'm a little teapot
Short and stout (Stand with hands out to side and knees bent),
Here is my handle (Put hand on hip),
Here is my spout (Extend opposite hand curved and into the air).
When I get all steamed up
Then I shout,
"Just tip me over and pour me out!" (Tip body to the side as if being poured.)

Repeat.

Things to watch for: Look for little signs of the children's personal creativity. As they become familiar with the song they will be different kinds of "teapots."

Old MacDonald Had A Farm

Record: Put out by many companies or may be sung by class.

Age Level: Two-and-a-half years and older.

Purpose: Teaches the children various animals and their corresponding sounds. It develops large and small muscles depending on the type of animal chosen. Make it funny by saying animals such as an elephant or tiger is on the farm or sing "He had a *duck*—with a moo-moo here." The children love the confusion and yell "No, a duck goes quack, quack." Some very quick children will catch onto the game and try to confuse the teacher by saying, "He had a *lamb*, with an oink, oink here."

Verses: Old MacDonald had a farm
Eee-i, Eee-i-O!
And on that farm he had a _____ (pig, cow, duck, snake, bird, chicken, horse, mouse).
Eee-i, Eee-i-O.
With a ------, ------ here (whatever sound the chosen animal makes)
and a ------, ----- there,
Here a ------,
There a ------,
Everywhere a ------, ------.
Old MacDonald had a farm
Eee-i, Eee-i-O!

(Whenever an animal is chosen, have the children act it out and make the sound that the animal makes, i.e., chicken: walk in semi-squatting position with elbows bent and hands on waist, waving elbows back and forth, saying "cluck, cluck.")

Things to watch for: Watch for creativity of the animals chosen and how the children act them out, i.e., will they all look and move in the same manner when being a cat or dog?

Loobey Loo

Age Level: Three years and older.

Purpose: Use parts of the body unfamiliar to the children. It is a good teaching device for educating them in human anatomy.

Organization: Circle formation, going clockwise with hands joined.

Chorus: Repeat after each verse:

> Here we go loobey loo,
> Here we go loobey light,
> Here we go loobey loo,
> All on a Saturday night. (Children move in a circle formation for chorus.)

Verses: I put my right hand in

> I take my right hand out,
> I give my hand a shake, shake, shake and turn myself about. (On verse children stand still, facing the center and follow directions of song. On "turn myself about" they make a complete circle in place, then get ready to join hands and skip or slide around in a circle for chorus.)
> I put my elbows in, etc.
> I put my thumbs in, etc.
> I put my tummy in, etc.
> I put my head in, etc.
> End with, I put my whole self in, etc. (Shake all parts of the body vigorously.)

Things to watch for: Getting the smaller children back to circle formation for the chorus may present a problem. This writer makes a game of it by humming loudly "Ohhh............" until all have joined hands.

Three Blind Mice

Age Level: Three-and-a-half years and older.

Purpose: Being able to quickly follow commands and change direction.

Organization: Children join hands in circle formation and move clockwise.

Verses: Three blind mice,
    Three blind mice,
    See how they run (Circle),
    See how they run,
    They all ran after the farmer's wife (All drop hands and run after previously chosen "farmer's wife"),
    She cut off their tails with a carving knife (She then chases them and they run from her).
    Did you ever see such a sight in your life (Join hands again on last line of "Three Blind Mice"),
    As three blind mice.

Things to watch for: The instructor should set spatial limitations for the chasing sequence.

Little Sally Saucer

Age Level: Four years and older.

Purpose: This game is fun and teaches an early form of sportsmanship. It is also helpful in teaching a child patience. Most of the children will want to be "Sally" but will have to wait until they are chosen.

Organization: The children join hands in a circle formation moving clockwise with one child as "Sally" sitting in the middle.

Verses: Little Sally Saucer
    Sitting in a saucer,
    Cry Sally, cry Sally,
    Wipe away your tears Sally.
    Turn to the East, Sally
    Turn to the West, Sally.
    Turn to the one that you love best!
    ("Sally" sits and rubs her eyes as if crying. She dries away the tears. "Sally" shuts her eyes tightly and turns with her finger pointing and arm extended to one side, then around to the other side and then stops. Whomever she is pointing at is the next "Sally.")

Things to watch for: Make sure the children going around "Sally" don't yell out, thus enabling her to point at specific children. It will take away the fun of being chosen.

Bingo

Age Level: Four years and older.

Purpose: It incorporates two different activities to a rhythmical pattern.

Organization: Circle formation moving clockwise with hands joined.

Verses: There was a farmer had a dog
And Bingo was his name-o
The farmer's dog's at our back door,
Begging for a bone-o.
B – I – N – G – O
B – I – N – G – O
B – I – N – G – O
And Bingo was his name-o.

Repeat.

(Have children sing song while moving in a circle. When spelling the name, have them stop, face the center of the circle, and clap out the letters.)

Variations: Have children face a partner (decided on ahead of time) and clap hands together when saying letters. Have them hook elbows with partner and swing around. (Not recommended unless children are four or five years old).

Things to watch for: There may be confusion when switching from a circle formation to standing still and clapping. See if they can clap on the beat (letter), not sooner or later (most will come in later).

Farmer In The Dell

Record: Put out by many companies, or may be sung by class.

Age Level: Four years and older.

Purpose: This song teaches the learning of long verses and moving as a group with individual participation. At the end children must go back to the circle formation.

Organization: Circle formation moving clockwise with hands joined.

Verses: The farmer in the dell,
The farmer in the dell,
Hi-o the dairy-o,
The farmer in the dell.

(One child stands in circle as "farmer" while the others skip around him.)

The farmer takes a wife,
The farmer takes a wife,
Hi-o the dairy-o,
The farmer takes a wife.

(The farmer chooses one of the children to be his wife and they hold hands. The rest of the children circle around them.)

The wife takes the nurse,
The wife takes the nurse,
Hi-o the dairy-o,
The wife takes the nurse.

(This continues with each new person taking another until they reach the cheese.)

The nurse takes the child, etc.
The child takes the dog, etc.
The dog takes the cat, etc.
The cat takes the mouse, etc.
The mouse takes the cheese, etc.
The cheese stands alone

(Then they all go back to the circle and move around the cheese).

Things to watch for: If the group is too small, this song should be eliminated. There must be at least ten children to make it fun for all. (In the count of ten exclude the teacher).

The Sesame Street Book And Record

Record: Columbia Stereo CS 1069, Original Cast. The album contains eighteen songs with a picture book and song sheet. It is a marvelous instrument in getting the children to act out all types of characters and movements. Since so many children are familiar with the television program, they will feel very comfortable with the album, whether listening and sitting or acting it out. Some of the selections that this writer has found to be particularly helpful and amusing are:

Side I: # 3 — "I've Got Two."
         # 4 — "Going for a Ride."
         # 6 — "Everybody Wash."
         # 8 — "Up and Down."
Side II: # 4 — "J-Jump."
         # 5 — "People in Your Neighborhood."
         # 6 — "Rub Your Tummy."
         # 10 — "Rubber Duckie."

Figure 20. The song Rub . . .

Figure 21. . . . Your Tummy.

The children can interpret the activities and characters as they wish, going from the very simple to the complex. It teaches the children parts of the body, familiar characters, and big muscle movement and makes the imaginary become real.[4]

GAMES USING RHYTHMIC BACKGROUND

A number of interesting games may be performed to music. In the main, they are a variety of one theme: stopping the music. Some of these are similar to the old favorite game of *Musical Chairs*.

Freeze

Children pair off. On the start of a record they run from their partner. When the music stops, they must quickly find their partner and sit on the floor. The last pair to find each other and sit are "out." Have them join the teacher and become "judges."

Statues

Have children either follow a leader or work individually. When the music is played they can run, skip, roll, hop, or jump. As the music stops they must hold their position without

Figure 22. The Tire Roll. (Refer to page 201.)

falling. The teacher may continue the game as long as she likes, eliminating the children that fall if she desires.

Notes to Chapter 4

1. Mollie S. Smart and Russell C. Smart, *Children, Development, and Relationships*, rev. ed. (New York: Macmillan, 1972).
2. Committee of California School Supervisors Association, *Guiding the Young Child* (Boston: D. C. Heath, 1959).
3. Adapted from Marian Anderson, Margaret E. Elliot, and Jenne LaBerge, *Play with a Purpose: Elementary School Physical Education* (New York: Harper & Row, 1972).
4. Obtained by written permission of Jon Stone, Executive Director, Children's Television Workshop, 1 Lincoln Plaza, New York, New York 10023.

Chapter 5

Physical Fitness And Exercises

It is erroneous to assume that a physical education class implies exercising alone. A complete program should incorporate exercises along with games, apparatus work, tumbling, rhythms, and movement exploration. The class should include a five minute warm-up period, essential for stretching and flexing the muscles. Proper exercising is only a small part of fitness.

PHYSICAL FITNESS

Physical fitness includes two important factors. The first emphasizes the health of each child; the second incorporates a sound program of physical activity in daily life that will remain with the youngster through adulthood.

Most children are more active than adults. It is pathetic that many adults forget the necessity of physical activity, and that what comes naturally to the child is work for the adult. If a youngster can be more physically aware of himself, and find a program from which he attains rewards, he will hopefully continue in the same vein throughout adulthood.

Today many people are aware of the need for physical fitness. In 1954 Dr. Hans Kraus compared certain strength and flexibility measurements of 4,000 New York City children with the same number of Central European students. He was trying to discover why so many of his patients, of middle age and older, had lower-back ailments. Could there be causal·factors among children? According to his findings, 57 percent of the American children failed one or more of the tested items (Five dealing with strength, one with flexibility) while Austrian, Swiss, and Italian children failed only 9 percent.[1] The public was unaware of the limitations of Dr. Kraus's study, which excluded endurance testing and included only one flexibility test. The conclusions were drawn primarily from strength testing. An additional omission was a child's life style—his cultural background. Generally speaking, a child reared in an agrarian setting would have more strength and endurance due to his work load, while a child of suburbia, whose parents expected less strenuous work, would probably not be as physically fit. If the study had incorporated tests for endurance, agility, flexibility, and strength and had considered cultural differences, the results might have been more accurate. Nonetheless, the American press made a tremendous issue of Dr. Kraus's study concerning the lack of fitness of American children, and it led to the establishment of President Eisenhower's Youth Fitness Committee. The Committee, now known as the President's Council on Fitness and Sport, continued through the Kennedy and Johnson eras, and had far-reaching effects on the quality of school physical education programs.

The importance of physical fitness can be seen in the following points:

1. Fitness improves general health and is essential for full living.
2. Fitness aids in weight control. The number one killer in America is heart disease, which can be partially guarded against by proper diet and the reduction of weight. The heart works more efficiently when made to perform more vigorously. It is a muscle and, as with all muscles, increases in size and strength with use. The more it is asked to perform, the stronger it grows. If the heart has been commanded to do little for years and is suddenly expected to perform vigorously, it can't respond as you demand. This is why a fitness program should be developed and increased slowly.
3. Fitness aids in tension release. As one matures and takes on more responsibilities, new "headaches" are created.

Recreation and physical activity allow for a temporary change of scene and of daily habits.

4. Regular activity stimulates growth and development. Muscles are strengthened, making for more efficient and enjoyable movement. A fit body uses less energy to perform tasks, thus leading to an increase in that body factor known as vitality.[2]

5. Exercise improves a child's or adult's self-image. As a rule, people look the way they feel; their mental attitude is shown in their appearance. If one is depressed or unhappy, the body will slouch and sag. If one feels good, the body will be more erect. Frequently we get into a "fatigue rut." The less we do, the harder it is to get going. Once this is recognized and changed, a person will have more energy gained through added activity.

There are definite physical areas that can be developed through fitness. Some of these are: strength (through large muscle activity); endurance (ability to carry on an activity for a period of time); agility (change of direction with good control); flexibility (range of movements of the joints); coordination (harmonious movement of the muscles); and balance (maintaining body equilibrium in various positions).

The late President John F. Kennedy, himself a fitness advocate, stated that "The physical vigor of our citizens is one of America's most precious resources. If we waste or neglect this resource, if we allow it to dwindle or grow soft, then we will destroy much of our ability to meet the great and vital challenges which confront our people."[3]

EXERCISES

A good warm-up period will include exercises that develop balance, strength, and coordination, to name but a few. It is imperative to remember the age of the group with which the teacher is dealing.

Following directions and working in groups will be a new experience for many of the children. Learning commands that adults consider basic will open up an entirely unfamiliar vocabulary to the youngster. Examples might be *forward, backward, circle formation,* and *V-sit.* The children will be expected to make muscles perform that have never been used. It is a complicated task as can be seen in the next sequence:

Figure 23. Warm-up exercises develop balance . . .

Figure 24. . . . strength, and coordination.

1. The teacher asks the children to stand in front of her with legs apart, extending their arms and turning about, making sure they are touching no one.
2. She then demonstrates a windmill, which the children are asked to imitate. The exercise is performed by alternating the left hand across the body to the right foot, standing tall, and then bringing the right hand across to the left foot. The legs must be kept straight.

3. Most of the children, even after seeing the teacher's demonstration, will do at least one of the following three things: (1) bend their knees; (2) bring their right hand to the right leg; (3) stay in a bent position and swing the arms back and forth from toe to toe.

Corrections should be made tactfully when the child performs incorrectly in order to develop (1) proper direction-following and (2) good muscle coordination. Note: If a child has performed the best to his ability and yet cannot achieve the required results, he is probably not ready for that skill but at least he has had the opportunity and exposure to try something new. It is the quality of effort and performance, not the quantity, that count. The reason for the emphasis on quality is analogous to the work of a diamond cutter. If a cutter is slightly off, he can change a gem's value. Similarly, if an exercise is slightly off, it may use muscles that will not aid a student to acquire a particular skill or area the teacher is trying to develop. It is this writer's opinion that most young children are physically and emotionally ready to perform simple exercises.

The Importance Of Good Posture

Posture is the way in which the whole body is balanced, not only in sitting and standing, but also in play and at rest. It is achieved through good muscle tone and healthy skeletal development as well as through general physical and mental health.[4] Correct posture is the core of normal behavior. The ability to withstand gravitation and to get out into space determines the range of experience. If a child or adult is unable to have a full range of physical articulation, he will have restricted mobility.[5]

The best time to develop good posture is when the child's body is still forming and growing. Many problems such as sagging stomachs, lower-back problems, and sloping shoulders in adult life are a result of poor body alignment. It is common to see a woman with curved shoulders and a protruding abdomen caused by improper alignment of the pelvic girdle. Another illustration is the extremely tall girl who bends the knees and stands with her weight on one foot with the hip extended. She wonders why she has back problems when married and pregnant. Good posture must be taught at an early age and constantly encouraged until the youngster reaches maturity.

Exercises For Improving Posture

Note: Ages listed after each exercise are the recommended ages for *introducing* each task. All of the listed exercises may be done by older children as well.

Stomach Exercises
(To Reduce Protruding Abdomen and Sway Back)

1. *V-Sit* (Four years and older)

   a. Sit with the knees bent and the feet flat on the floor. Place hands on the floor behind the back, raising feet and straightening the legs. Extend the arms toward the feet and hold. The body forms a *V* and the arms are used for balance. Repeat four times.

   b. This is more difficult than (a). Slowly lower the arms and legs simultaneously while looking at the feet.
   c. Combine lowering and raising to a *V* sit from a lying position by flinging the arms over the head and the legs up to the arms. (Four-and-a-half or five years and older.)

2. *Angry Cat* (Three-and-a-half years and older)

   Start on hands and knees. Look toward tummy. Slowly lift up tummy by pulling it in and arch back at the same time. Count to five to achieve arch, hold for five counts and relax for five. Repeat seven times.

3. *Leg Lifts* (Recommended for those children with good abdominal strength—this shouldn't be attempted before five years of age.)

   Lie on back. Place hands under small of the back (top of rear end). Keep legs straight and slowly lift until legs are perpen-

dicular to the body. Then slowly lower legs. Repeat five times down and up.

Exercises For The Back

1. *Climb Fireman's Pole* (Three-and-a-half years and older)

Start in semi-squatting position. Move arms upward as if climbing pole and extend until on tiptoes, still reaching higher and higher. This exercise is good also for balance. Repeat five times.

2. *Rocking Horse* (Three-and-a-half years and older)

Lie on tummy. Bend knees and hold the feet. Rock back and forth on tummy by pulling legs and lifting the chest. Repeat ten times.

Figure 25.
The V-Sit.

Figure 26. Leg Lift.

Exercises For Neck And Upper Back

1. *Neck Stretch* (Two-and-a-half years and older)

Lie on back. Lift head only and look at toes, lowering head until flat on floor. Continue for a count of ten and build up to twenty.

2. *Frog* (Two-and-a-half years and older)

Sit on floor with back straight. Rest head back on upper shoulder blades. Bring bottom jaw to upper lip. Repeat twenty times.

3. *Shoulder Lift* (Two-and-a-half years and older)

Sitting Indian-style (cross-legged) with back straight, lift shoulders up and down. Then move shoulders forward and back; then alternate shoulders going back and forward. Make circles with the shoulders. Teacher: Put on a record with a drum beat. Try to have the youngsters use shoulders to beat of the record, and make a game of follow the leader.

Exercises For Feet
(Two-and-a-half years and older)

1. *Tiptoe* (to strengthen calves, arch, toes, and balls of feet)

Standing tall with arms extended, go slowly up on tiptoes (good test of balance) and slowly down (also develops muscles known as the hamstrings, in back of legs). Repeat ten times. The teacher may suggest that the children alternate feet: while one is going up, the other is going down.

2. *Marble Pickup* (Two-and-a-half years and older)

Place any small object on the floor, such as a marble or pencil. Pick it up with the toes and place it again on the floor. Repeat five times.

3. *Towel Pull* (Two-and-a-half years and older)

Two children face each other gripping a towel or rope with the toes. On a given signal, pull until there is a winner. Repeat.

4. *Walking* (Three-and-a-half years and older)

Walk on a line, first with toes pointing inward, then outward, then with toes pointing straight ahead. This will be extremely difficult for the youngster to master; he will need much individual attention as the foot muscles are not well developed. The muscles have never been "told" by the brain to perform this task. Walk around the room two or three times to develop this skill. (Use adhesive or masking tape on the floor as a substitute for lines if necessary.)

5. *Combination Of Tiptoe And Walking*

Walk—walk—tiptoe—tiptoe. Any combination will do to a drum beat. This is excellent for arch development and balance. Have at least twenty repetitions.

Warm-up Exercises For Strength, Flexibility, Balance

Note: Ages in parenthesis are the recommended ages for beginning each exercise. All exercises included are utilized by adults as well as children.

Caterpillar (Two-and-a-half years and older)

Stand up straight. Then bend at the waist, putting hands to the floor and walking outward with the hands until lying on the tummy. Next, put the weight on the hands and feet and have feet walk to hands. Repeat five times.

Note: When hands are moving, feet should be firmly planted on the floor. The same holds true when feet are walking: hands must be still.

Things to watch for: Children will have a tendency to move hands and feet simultaneously as in a *Dog Walk*. (Don't correct the child until he is four on this activity.)

Areas of development: Upper arm strength, leg muscle development, hamstring stretch.

Toe Touch (Two-and-a-half years and older)

Stand erect and bend from the pelvic area, touching toes with the hands. Heels should be planted firmly on the ground. Teacher: Make sure children don't bend from the waist; bending from the waist doesn't allow for flexibility of the back. To accomplish this, have the youngsters place their hands on their hip bones, bending from the hips. Repeat ten times.

Things to watch for: The children will have a tendency to (1) bend from the waist and (2) bend the knees.

Areas of development: Hamstring stretch and balance development.

Bounce (Two-and-a-half years and older)

The stride-stand position is taken. With feet remaining on the floor, bounce from the waist to the floor, placing the palms in front of the body, in between the legs, and through the legs behind the heels. Repeat ten times in sets of three.

Things to watch for: Bending from the hips and keeping the legs straight while bouncing is essential. If children can't reach the floor, have them put their legs farther apart.

Front   Middle   Back (through legs in stride stand)

  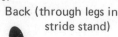

Areas of development: Hamstring stretch and balance development.

Head Circles (Two-and-a-half years and older)

Sitting cross-legged with the hands in the lap, circle the head slowly touching top of the shoulders, upper shoulder blades, and top of the chest with the chin. Repeat three times in each direction.

Side   Back   Side   Front

Things to watch for: Children will have a tendency to be stiff and not let their heads rotate on the neck. If done too fast, they may get dizzy. Make sure the exercise is performed slowly, with eyes shut.

Areas of development: The neck muscles are strengthened and flexibility is increased.

Arm Circles (Two-and-a-half years and older)

Stand in erect position with back straight extending the arms to sides of the body. Make large circles with the arms, using bent knees for balance and freedom of movement. Make middle-sized circles followed by small circles. Repeat, going from small to middle to large circles in counts of five each, building up to ten.

Things to watch for: Children will frequently circle the wrists rather than the full arms, especially when doing small circles. Telling them to keep arms stiff prevents this problem.

Areas of development: Upper arm muscles are strengthened (through keeping arms in the air for such a long period) and flexibility of the ball and socket joint through rotation is developed. The exercise also develops the shoulder area, and helps children with a tendency for sloping shoulders.

Note: This exercise can also strengthen the back if done in a sitting position. When children are performing the large circles counterclockwise, the teacher can tell if the entire joint range is being used by watching the corner of the upper lip which should go up.

Swim (Two-and-a-half years and older)

Bend at the waist in a stride-stand and move arms as if doing the crawl. Repeat at right side and left side ten times each.

Figure 27. The Swim . . .

Figure 28. . . . develops arm, shoulder,
and hamstring muscles.

Things to watch for: Since many youngsters don't know how to swim at this young age, they may do a dog paddle. Make sure they bend the elbows and lift the arms before reaching forward. The teacher should say "Reach—reach" as the exercise is being performed. Swim ten times in all directions.

Areas of development: The arm, shoulder, and hamstring muscles are being developed. This is an excellent waist-trimmer.

Run In Place (Two-and-a-half years and older)

Stand erect and run in place, with little steps, five times, then lift knees up high and run in place five times. Arms may be extended at sides for balance. Repeat sets (small to large) five times.

Count: Small - two - three - four - five - up - two - three - four - five.
Small - two - three - four - five - up - two - three - four - five.

Things to watch for: Large kicks or runs may not be high enough and may look more like little jumps. Emphasize lifting the knee as in a fast march.

Areas of development: The arches, leg muscles, and heart (through vigorous movement) are strengthened.

Trunk Twist (Three years and older)

Stand with hands on hips in bent position and twist forward, to the right side, to the back, and to the left side. Perform the circle three times in each direction.

Things to watch for: Many youngsters will not bend back far enough. Suggest that they bend their knees slightly and look back over their heads.

Areas of development: Coordination and balance; also a waist-trimmer for the heavier child.

"Eight" (Four years and older)

1. Stand tall with the feet together.
2. Continually moving the feet apart, turn feet out, then in, to the count of eight until the legs end up in the stride-stand (legs apart).
3. Put the arms high above the head and climb down an imaginary pole to the count of eight leaving heels flat on the floor (stretches the hamstring muscles).
4. Place the hands on the floor with the feet firmly planted and walk out with the hands to a count of eight.
5. Walk back to the feet with the hands to an eight-count.
6. Climb up an imaginary pole with the hands for an eight-count.

7. Move the feet back from a stride stand—toes pointing in, rotating to heel until the feet are together for an eight-count.
8. Repeat twice, making the count faster and faster.

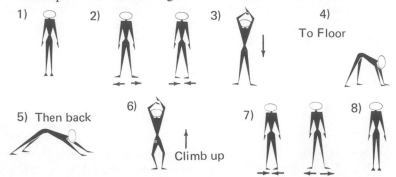

Note: Children three to four years of age will not do this complex exercise precisely but what counts are the attempt and the fun of doing it.

Things to watch for: Children will have difficulty toeing feet out and in. The teacher may have to place their feet in order for them to understand the exercise. The youngsters will also have the tendency to walk like a dog on all fours rather than leave the feet firmly planted.

Areas of development: This exercise teaches the children many things such as coordination, agility, direction-following, and balance. As an added bonus, it teaches them how to count to eight.

Sprinter (Three-and-a-half years and older)

Squat with the weight on the palms. The left leg is then fully extended. Alternate the position of the legs by jumping and lifting the hips. Repeat five times.

Things to watch for: Feet may slide in changing position rather than being lifted by hips.

Areas of development: Coordination, stretching, and flexibility are all utilized in this exercise. The areas that are strengthened are the leg and arm and shoulder muscles.

Windmills (Four and five years)

Stand with legs apart (stride-stand), arms extended to the sides of the body, alternate the right hand across to left foot, and rise to standing position. This is continued with the left hand going across to the right foot. Repeat ten times.

Things to watch for: Children may bend their legs, not alternate arms with legs, and move arms to feet without returning to standing position in between.

Areas of development: Excellent for stretching, flexibility, and coordination. In older children, it is a good waist-trimmer.

Figure 29. The Windmill.

Jumping Jacks (Four and five-year-olds; two-and-a-half-year-olds can try to jump)

Stand erect with hands at sides. While bringing the hands over the head and clapping with straight arms, the feet jump out to the sides forming an inverted *V*. Jump again, returning to the original position. Repeat ten times.

Things to watch for: Youngsters will have a tendency to jump up and down without spreading their legs or will forget to raise hands above their bodies.

Areas of development: Excellent for developing coordination, balance, and leg strength.

Sit-Ups (Four to five years and older)

Lie on the floor with the knees bent. (A straight-leg sit-up can eventually harm the back muscles, while bent-leg sit-ups strengthen the abdominal muscles.) Arms are extended above the head. Fling the arms overhead and touch the toes, then

Figure 30. The Sit-Up.

uncurl the back to the original position. Repeat five times and work up to ten repetitions.

Note: More muscularly advanced students (usually school-age) will be able to sit up with hands clasped behind their heads. Repeat five times and work up to ten repetitions.

Things to watch for: Feet have a natural tendency to rise off the floor until the abdominal muscles are developed. Have children work in pairs with one child sitting on feet (back toward child doing the exercise) of the child performing the exercise. The children may also use elbows to aid in sitting up. Encourage children *not* to do this since it won't develop the stomach area.

Area of development: Abdominal muscles.

Sit-Backs

Sit on the floor with knees fully bent. Lean back a few inches and hold. (For a complete discussion refer to *Total Fitness in 30 Minutes a Week* by Morehouse and Gross.)

Chinese Get-Up (Four years and older)

This is a double exercise as well as a stunt. Have children work in pairs of approximately equal weight. They will sit back to back, hooking elbows, with bent knees and feet flat on floor. At the count of three have them push their backs together, rising to a standing position. Repeat twice.

Steps *Forward*
with Right Foot

Steps *Backward*
with Right Foot

This exercise may be further developed by having the youngsters raise half-way (weight is on thighs) and try to walk in the same direction. Have them decide before they start which direction they will head and on what foot they'll step first. This results in one walking forward while the other is going backward. They should use the same feet in order to maintain

Figure 31. Chinese Get-Up.

balance. This is an excellent exercise for developing coordination and will be accomplished only by very physically advanced students.

Things to watch for: There is a great tendency for children to lean forward, pulling their partner onto their backs rather than pushing the backs together and using force against their feet. Make sure children are of relatively equal weight to prevent this from happening.

Areas of development: Thigh muscles are greatly developed as are balance and coordination.

Push-Up (Five years and older)

Put weight on top of knees and hands in prone position (facing floor) with back straight. Bend the elbows and let the body nearly touch to the floor, then push back up to straight arm position. Repeat five times.

A more advanced form, the full-body push-up, has the entire weight on hands and toes in prone position. Repeat five times.

Things to watch for: Children have not developed arm strength and therefore will lie on stomach rather than keeping trunk off the floor.

Areas of development: The upper and lower arm and shoulder muscles are strengthened.

Yoga Exercises For Children
(Recommended for youngsters three to five years and older)

1. *The Cat*

The child kneels down with the palms flat on the floor and the head lowered. He arches his back, then sinks the back down and raises a leg while looking at it.

Things to watch for: The preschooler (age two-and-a-half to three-and-a-half) will generally not be able to arch and lower the back, since the muscles required to do that skill are not fully developed.

Areas of development: Complete body stretch, strengthening back muscles.

2. *The Bird*

The children stand on tiptoes, bend slightly at the waist, and extend their arms behind the body while spreading the fingers.

Things to watch for: The two-and-a-half- to three-and-a-half-year-old may not be able to maintain balance. Have the youngsters "fly" around the room once they have held the position even it it's momentary.

Areas of development: Improves posture and balance; strengthens feet and ankles.

3. *The Stork*

The children stand on one foot, bend the other leg behind them, and place hands together as if they were praying. Suggest they alternate feet.

Things to watch for: The two-and-a-half- to three-and-a-half-year-old will generally need support against a wall or aid from a partner.

Areas of development: Balance and concentration are developed in this exercise.

4. *The Rabbit*

The youngsters kneel on the ground and place their heads on the floor in front of the knees. The arms are stretched and hands grasp the ankles.

Things to watch for: If the children go into this exercise too fast it may turn into a forward roll.

Area of development: Spinal column stretch.

5. *Swallow*

This exercise is similar to the *Rabbit* except that the body is fully lowered, allowing the buttocks to be placed on the feet.

The arms are stretched forward and the head is on the floor in front of the knees.

Things to watch for: Relatively few mistakes will be seen even when the exercise performed by the youngest of pre-schoolers.

Area of development: Complete body stretch.

6. *The Fish*

Ask the class to lie facing the floor. The hands are placed at shoulder level and the arms are pushed into a straight position. The head is tipped back and the lips are brought together and apart (fish kiss).

Things to watch for: Some youngsters will need help in straightening the arms. Many will keep the weight on their elbows.

Areas of development: Spinal column stretch; strengthens lower back.

7. *The Circle*

Ask the youngsters to kneel and reach back, grasping their ankles while looking backwards.

Figure 32.
The Circle,
a yoga exercise.

Things to watch for: Some children will lose all sense of balance when their heads are tipped back. Have them do this exercise slowly to prevent falling to the side.

Area of development: Spinal column stretch.

8. *The Swan*

This is similar to the *Fish* except the legs are bent and the feet try to touch the head.

Feet Touching Head

Up

Things to watch for: Many children will not be flexible enough to properly perform the *Swan*.

Areas of development: Strengthens abdomen and stretches spinal column.

Suggested Plan For Exercises

It is important to remember that young children fatigue easily and have a short attention span. They will be expected to use the mind and body in performing exercises; therefore, the program should not be too rigorous. The warm-up periods should include exercises for many different parts of the body. Following are two possible plans the teacher may use:

1. Warm-up: *Jumping Jacks* (ten times).
   Head: *Head Circles* (three in each direction).
   Arms: *Arm Circles* (five times each size and in each direction).
   Trunk: *Trunk Twist* (three times in each direction).
   Stomach: *Sit-Ups* (three times).
   Legs: *Sprinter* (five times).

or

2. Warm-up: *Run In Place* (five times, small and large steps).
   Shoulders: *Shoulder Lift* (any number of times).
   Waist: *Swim In Place* (ten times in each direction).
   Legs: *Chinese Get-Up* (twice).
   Feet: *Tiptoes* (alternate feet ten times).

There are numerous ways that exercise programs can be handled. The two examples above are only personal suggestions. Have the youngsters take turns leading the group as they become familiar with the exercises. It gives them early leadership experience, develops confidence with groups, and aids them in remembering the skills taught.

Notes to Chapter 5

1. Victor P. Dauer and Robert P. Pangrazi, *Dynamic Physical Education for Elementary School Children*, 5th ed. (Minneapolis, Minnesota: Burgess Publishing Company, 1975).
2. Ibid.
3. John F. Kennedy, "The Soft America," *Sports Illustrated* 26 December, 1960.
4. Mollie S. Smart and Russell C. Smart, *Children, Development, and Relationships*, rev. ed. (New York: Macmillan, 1972).
5. Pearl M. Rosborough, *Physical Fitness and the Child's Reading Problem* (New York: Exposition Press, 1963).

Chapter 6

Homemade Apparatus And Small Equipment

The use of apparatus is a beneficial and practical part of the young child's physical education program. The problem with many text books is that they teach specific skills that can be performed only on expensive equipment. Our YMCA has been in existence for only five years, and there is no conceivable way we can afford the luxuries of a $300 balance beam or a $500 trampoline. We are a typical example, not an exception. Most day-care centers, nursery schools, and kindergartens have limited budgets.

The following chapter will demonstrate activities with variations that can be performed on home-made, inexpensive equipment or apparatus that can be gathered through donations and yard sales or made using creativity and a little ingenuity.

GUIDELINES

There are essential guidelines that are recommended when any piece of equipment or apparatus is used:

1. The class should stand in front of the teacher when she is demonstrating a skill performed on the apparatus.
2. Progression should be adjusted to the ability level of each class.

3. Spotting is essential. Under normal conditions a teacher should not "lift" a child completely through a stunt. She may assist, but should not do it for him.
4. The children must have complete faith in the instructor.
5. Every child should participate. Frequently the anxious children will move to the background, letting the enthusiastic youngsters take charge.
6. Work individually with each child until he can accomplish what is expected for his own ability. Relate to every child. Have patience and understanding.
7. Look for hidden handicaps. One child's foot may turn decidedly inward when he is walking on the balance beam; another child may turn his elbow outward when catching a ball. Inform the parents of minor problems and suggest that they have the more noticeable handicaps checked by a doctor. For example, one of my youngsters had a problem with depth perception. When a ball was thrown, he could not judge the distance and kept his arms extended, hoping the ball would land in his hands. His mother, when told of the situation, had a consultation with a pediatrician. He performed a thorough eye examination and found there was a problem with the left eye. This youngster now wears a patch on his good eye (to strengthen the weak one) for a number of hours a day. An instructor has to be keenly aware of the children and look for any unusual changes they may exhibit.
8. Occasionally ask a parent to assist with the lesson. (This is strictly a personal preference.) Many parents wish to help their youngsters at home on a jungle gym or swing set but don't know how to spot. This writer has found the parents very eager to learn. Their enthusiasm spreads to the home environment, thus incorporating skills into the child's daily life.
9. Stress safety: Remove glasses, empty pockets, tie shoelaces, wear comfortable clothing, and work with mats.
10. The instructor should consider the following criteria when choosing equipment to be utilized in the class:
    a. Does it develop balance?
    b. Does it teach coordination?
    c. Does it help teach your objectives?
    d. Will it be enjoyable for the children?

    e. Will it develop strength; will it build up endurance?

    f. Can it develop flexibility and agility?

11. Help each child develop self-confidence. Many will have an innate fear of the unknown. It should be the instructor's objective to make every experience positive and exciting. Personal satisfaction comes from giving each child a happy, purposeful experience. If his "hang-ups" are ignored or reinforced, the instructor has fallen short of the final goal.

APPARATUS AND SMALL EQUIPMENT

All of the apparatus and small equipment listed below is for the young child's use. Each piece should be modified or expanded depending upon the ability level of each child. A firm rule cannot be made; a three-year-old may be far more advanced in certain areas than a four-year-old. The reverse may also hold true.

Ropes	Small Balance Beam
Hanging Rope	Sawhorses
Balls	Sawhorses and Plank
Cones	Stegel
Dumbbells	Ladder
Banana	Jungle Gym
Tires	Maze System

Ropes

Type used: Clothesline rope made from a cotton blend is the best type for the young child's class. Most discount stores carry them at an inexpensive price. Nylon or plastic ropes tend to be too coarse. Have the rope approximately twenty feet in length.

Purposes and objectives:

1. The leg muscles are developed in most rope activities.
2. The children learn to follow directions, individually and as a group.
3. Rope work develops eye-foot coordination.
4. Timing: A child will learn where a rope must be before starting the jump; how high or low he must step to avoid hitting the rope; and how near or far to stand from a rope depending on whether it is stationary or moving. There are general rules that apply in answering the above questions

Figure 33. Low Water.

but essentially the youngster must establish his own approach.

Rope Activities

High Water

The rope is held high off the ground by the instructor and a helper (or tie the rope to a post, bar, or tree). The children line up in single file formation (or as a group in a horizontal line) and go under the rope without touching it. After the entire line has gone, the rope is lowered six inches. The same process is repeated until the rope is a few inches from the floor. Each child is given as many attempts as necessary to crawl under the rope.

Approaches

Children may lie on their backs either head or feet first or may crawl under the rope on their stomachs.

Low Water

The rope is slowly raised as the children jump over it. The spotter stands a few feet in front of the rope, grasping the shoulders of the children when the rope is raised and there is a

Figure 34. A child jumps . . .   *Figure 35. . . . over the rope . . .*

Figure 36. . . . in Low Water.

tendency to trip. The class should stand back, leaving room for a run before jumping.

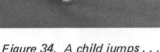

Snake

Snake is played in the same manner as *Low Water*, except that the rope is constantly moving back and forth like a wriggling snake. A spotter is essential since tripping may occur.

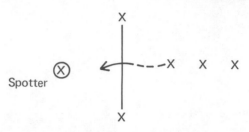

Jumping Rope (Recommended for children four years and older)

The children line up to see each other perform (this also eliminates boredom among the non-participants). The rope should sway from side to side, gently brushing the floor. The jumper must start his approach as the rope is coming toward him, leaping quickly over the rope and running toward the opposite side of the room. After the children can jump over the rope, *Follow The Leader* may be played. The next phase is to jump up and down as the rope swings back and forth. This is only a preliminary step in rope jumping—however, the pre-schooler should not be expected to progress any farther. He will not be able to jump in a stationary position with the rope turning completely over him.

The youngster may either: (1) jump with his feet together or (2) leap over the rope on one foot at a time, as in a running step.

Hanging Rope

Type used: A rope one to one-and-a-half inches wide for climbing purposes can be found in most sporting goods or home building-supply stores. Knot the rope around a ceiling brace or tree if it doesn't come equipped with a hook.

Purposes and objectives:

1. Rope hanging develops the upper trunk and arm muscles.
2. Coordination is developed.
3. Fear of heights can be overcome by jumping from the rope if the exercise is related to a fantasy figure such as Tarzan or Spiderman.

Note: Many young children should not be expected to climb the rope because their arm muscles are not well enough developed to hold the entire body weight. In considering a program of rope hanging skills the following points should be noted:

1. A chair is placed under the rope.
2. The rope hangs three to four feet off the floor; a double knot is tied at the base.
3. Each child reaches up to grasp the rope with the thumbs circling around and meeting the fingers.
4. Assist by lifting the child's buttocks, and helping him to cross his legs around the rope until he is sitting on the knot. The two-and-a-half-year-old may initially need the spotter to hold his hands and feet as he hasn't learned to control the thigh and arm muscles against the pull of gravity that is being applied to the total body weight.
5. While holding the child, gently sway the rope back and forth.

Figure 37. The child is helped onto the rope . . .

Figure 38.
. . . . sways back and forth . . .

Figure 39.
. . . and then swings by himself.

6. When the child's anxieties have disappeared, push the rope without holding him.
7. Ask the youngster to mount the rope with no assistance.
8. Once he can climb and swing by himself (usually not until the age of four or five), ask him to jump from the rope (kicking the legs out and releasing the hands) onto a mat.

Balls

Type used: Rubber playground balls six to eight inches in diameter should be purchased. These may be bought in any sporting goods store for two or three dollars apiece. Beachballs bounce poorly due to their lightness, but are good for hitting. An added bonus is their inexpensive price. Volleyballs are costly and hard.

Purposes and objectives:
1. Eye-hand coordination is finely developed in any type of ball handling such as bouncing, catching, throwing, or batting.

2. The sense of timing is developed. Each child will learn to answer his own questions about: (a) the length of time it takes for the rebound of the ball; and (b) the number of steps he will take when dribbling it.
3. The skill of accuracy and control of the ball's direction is learned through repetition and observation.

Ball Activities

Bouncing a Ball

1. Remember the age of the children. Many have never bounced a ball. Ask the youngsters to hold the ball in both hands, dropping it to the floor. When the ball rebounds, push it down again with a quick push. (Most children will bend to meet the ball, not waiting for the return.)
2. Once the children can bounce the ball with two hands, ask them to try the same skill with one hand. Remember their motor development. It will take many weeks before this can be achieved by the three-and-a-half to four-year-old, whose eye-hand coordination is not finely developed and for whom bouncing a ball is a difficult task. (See Figure 44.)
3. Ask the children to bounce the ball and walk forward. This is first accomplished by dropping the ball and catching it with both hands, stepping forward, and dropping it again. Moving in any direction requires the ball to be bounced in front and to the side of the foot that is back; for example the right hand pushes the ball to the right foot (back) when left foot is forward. Hands and feet work in opposition.

Run forward bouncing the ball, pivot (turn around), and bounce it back to the starting line.

4. Bounce the ball to a partner, pushing it out and down.

Catching a Ball

The children stand in a circle formation with the instructor in the middle. She throws the ball to each child. The youngster extends his arms and hands forward. Upon receiving the ball, he places his hands on the sides of it, pulling it close to his chest with the elbows pointing downward. (Some children will stick their elbows out to the side.)

After catching the ball, the child should throw it back to the teacher. If necessary, work individually with the children. This writer plays "catch" with each child before proceeding to other ball-handling skills. Make sure the child looks at the ball when catching it, not at the instructor. Any type of distraction will interfere with the progress of ball-handling.

Figure 40. Partners throwing and catching.

Figure 41. Catching a ball.

Passing a Ball

Once the ball has been passed around by the teacher, the children can throw it around or across the circle to each other.

Underhand Pass: The ball is held in both hands in front of and close to the body. The hands are lowered and the ball is pushed out and up. (There is a tendency to forget the *out*, which causes the ball to go straight up into the air.)

Overhand Pass: The ball is held with both hands close to the chest. The push is out and up from the chest (don't lower the ball to the legs). Make sure the elbows don't turn out.

Bounce Pass: The child faces a partner, pushes the ball from the chest, and aims it out and down (not straight down). The rebound is caught by the partner.

Use the passes in a game situation. Ask the children to form a circle with the teacher in the center. She may vary the passes, expecting the same in return, or can trick the children by not looking in their direction when throwing the ball. These variations should be attempted only by the more physically advanced youngsters.

Rolling a Ball

Ask the children to sit on the floor with legs apart and to push the ball with both hands (force should be evenly distributed and incorporate follow-through). This may also be performed as if one were bowling, where one hand releases the ball (feet in opposition to hands). Create a game situation by rolling the ball to a partner, along a line, at a target, or into a pail turned on its side.

Kicking a Ball

A ball may be kicked two ways: (1) with the toe, and (2) with the inside of the foot. The latter is recommended for accurate control over the direction the ball will take. Kicking a ball with the toe is incorrect, can injure the toe, and may ruin the ball.

The *Soccer* kick is accomplished by pushing the ball forward with the instep. Alternate the right with the left foot. The ball can be stopped by placing the foot on top of the ball. Practice going from one side of the room to the other for the soccer dribble.

Games Using The Variation Ball Skills:

Wonderball (see chapter 7): Passing.
Kickball (see chapter 7): Kicking and throwing.
Relay Races (see chapter 9): All the ball skills.
Monkey in the Middle (see chapter 7): Accuracy in catching and throwing.
Basket Toss (Recommended for children four years and older.): Divide the class into teams. Aim the ball into a wastebasket. Each "basket" is worth one point. The team with the most points in five minutes is the winner.
Cone Ball (For children four-and-a-half years and older.): Using cones as obstacles, bounce the ball around them (see *Relay Races*, chapter 9).
Pin Ball: Set up bowling pins (old plastic bottles) and try knocking them down with a rolling ball. Each child gets three turns.

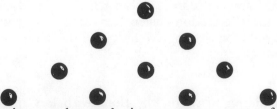

This exercise can be made into a team contest for children four-and-a-half to five.
Wall Ball: See chapter 7.

Cones

Type used: Cones stand approximately two inches high, are made of rubber, and can be brightly colored. They are used in road repair work and may be acquired from public works and transportation departments found in every town, or from sporting goods stores.
Purposes and objectives: Cones are generally used in obstacle races or drills to teach children coordination, change of direction, and balance.

Figure 42.
Careful one-handed dribble.

Figure 43.
Two hands "meeting" the ball.

Figure 44.
Confident one-handed dribble.

Figure 45. Dribbling around cones (notice different size balls).

Cone Activities

Cone Relays: (see chapter 9—*Relay Races*).

Dribbling Around Cones (Recommended for children five years and older).

An excellent method for teaching ball maneuverability is to place cones approximately four feet apart in a straight line. The children line up single file and dribble the balls to the side of each cone, going around the last cone and coming back in the same manner. The ball must bounce slightly ahead of the child.

Cone Pitch (Recommended for children four-and-a-half years and older.)

Cones are placed on their sides ten to fifteen feet from the player, the large ends facing the starting line. Each child must stand behind the starting line and roll a ball into the cone. Each "basket" is worth one point. This skill develops accuracy, eye-hand coordination, and control of the ball.

Dumbbells

Type used: They are usually made of wood, weigh approximately two pounds, are ten inches in length, and can be found in sporting goods stores at an inexpensive price. Dumbbells can be constructed by putting a styrofoam ball at each end of a stick.

Purposes and objectives: Dumbbells are used mainly in movement exploration activities. They develop eye-hand coordination, agility, and imagination. If a class were limited in its purchases of small equipment, this writer would recommend balls and dumbbells. Their use in creativity is unlimited.

Dumbbell Activities

Movement Exploration

A weight lifter: Be a "Strongman" (see fig. 8)
Marching: (see chapter 4). Be a: Baton twirler, Drummer, Fife or piccolo, Flag carrier.
Dog and *bone.*
Soldier and *gun.*
Sailor and *binoculars.* (Use dumbbells to represent italicized terms.)

Figure 46. Walking on tires with dumbbells.

Coordination Development

Ask the children to hold dumbbells while walking over tires. The dumbbells will prevent them from using their hands for balance by leaning over and touching the tires. (This should be performed *after* they can walk over the tires with ease.)

Banana

A banana is fairly easy to construct and has multiple uses. Two smooth, banana-shaped pieces of wood, approximately four by one-and-a-half feet, are placed side by side one to one-and-a-half feet apart. Five stairs are cut (four are one-and-a-half feet by five inches, and one is one-and-a-half feet by one foot) and are hammered across the inside of the "bananas" to join the two. The two narrower ones are on each side, the larger one on the bottom. Two rungs are hammered into place on the top-middle (flat side) of the "bananas."

Purposes and objectives: The banana is used as an initial step in teaching jumping from heights. It develops balance, eye-foot coordination, and agility.

Banana Activities

Movement Exploration

Rocking horse.
Boat.
Car.
Horse.

Climbing and Jumping

Ask the children to line up in single file formation with the spotter standing to the side of the banana.

Figure 47.

The Banana.

Overhead View

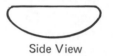
Side View

The following progression is suggested:

1. The youngsters crawl on their hands and knees up, over, and down the steps.
2. Ask them to walk up, over, and down the steps. Younger children have the tendency to stoop in maintaining their balance by holding on to the sides of the banana. The instructor should grasp one elbow of the performer to keep him erect.
3. Have the youngsters walk up and over the top step. On the last step they should jump, with both feet together, to the floor. The two-and-a-half to three-year-old will probably jump one foot at a time. The spotter should stand in front of the jumper, holding his hands and guiding him out and up until he lands on the floor. (Spotter bends down with the child.)
4. Gradually increase the height of jumping until the children can climb to the top step and jump without assistance, feet together for takeoff and landing with the knees slightly bent.

Pulling the Body Weight

Ask the class to lie on their stomachs with their legs "dead weight." Have them hold onto one step at a time, pulling their

Figure 48. Children rocking on the Banana.

bodies up the steps and dragging the legs (this develops upper trunk strength). The downward steps require the youngsters to "walk" with their hands, dragging the legs behind them. Make sure they don't use bent knees for support.

Tires

Type used: Most automobile shops or garages will donate old tires if asked. Paint them bright colors. Latex paint should be used as oil-base paint contains lead.

Purposes and objectives: Tires are extremely useful in developing balance, coordination, and agility. Rolling and controlling tires requires eye-hand coordination and arm strength.

Tire Activities

Crawling and Walking on Tires

The following progression is suggested:

1. Line the tires up, end to end in a zig-zag pattern. Ask each child to crawl on the tires without falling into the middle. The youngster should alternate the hands with the feet or he will roll off the tires onto the floor.

2. Once crawling has been achieved, ask the child to walk on the tires stepping on the rubber without falling off or into the middle. Many youngsters will fall forward to maintain their balance. The spotter should stand to one side, aiding the children who require help.
3. Add the use of dumbbells when they walk on the tires to develop coordination and balance.

Jumping Over Tires

1. The tires should remain in a zig-zag pattern. The spotter holds the wrist and lower arm of the jumper (this allows more control than if the hand is held). Each child jumps, with his feet together, from the inside of one tire to the next (from hole to hole). As the youngster jumps, the

Figure 49. Crawling and walking on tires.

spotter lifts his arm forward and up. Initially he will jump
one foot at a time. To aid in jumping, instruct the children
to lean slightly forward, bending their elbows and flexing
the knees. They should spring forward and up from the
balls of the feet.
2. Once each child has accomplished jumping with assistance,
   ask him to repeat the same skill while loosely holding the
   spotter's hand (this is more for security than balance).
3. Have him jump alone.

Movement Exploration

Tires can be used for:
Cars.
Horses.
Beds.
Houses.
Nests.

Rolling Tires

Ask each child to place a tire upright. Have him roll it across
a room and back. He should run along its side, pushing the top

Figure 50. Tire walking.

*Figure 51.
Jumping with assistance . . .*

*Figure 52.
. . . and alone.*

forward with the palm of the hand. He will learn from experience that if the tire is pushed to the side it will fall.

Relay Races

Rolling the tire can be incorporated into a relay race. Tires may also be used in obstacle relays, one in front of another approximately five feet apart.

Ball Skills Using Tires (Recommended for children four-and-a-half years and older)

Balls are dribbled around tires. This exercise can be used as a drill or it may take the form of a relay race.

Tires may serve as "baskets." They are placed five to ten feet in front of each player or team. The children may roll or gently toss the ball (if done roughly, the ball will bounce out of the tire) into the hole of the tire. Every "basket" is worth one point. This activity is excellent for developing accuracy and eye-hand coordination.

Small Balance Beam

Type used: A small balance beam is simple and inexpensive to construct. Go to any lumber yard and purchase one two-inch by four-inch by eight-foot beam. Nail it onto three blocks of wood (two-inch by four-inch by six-inch) for stability. The two end blocks should be perpendicular to the beam. Sand it down and paint it a bright color.

Purposes and objectives: Balance beam work develops coordination and balance. It strengthens the foot muscles and teaches children to walk with even weight distribution. This piece of apparatus is necessary before attempting skills on higher beams.

Balance Beam Activities

A program for teaching beam work should follow these suggested steps:

1. The children line up in single file with the spotter standing to one side of the beam. Since the beam is only two inches from the floor, no mats are required. Each child walks across the beam with one foot directly in front of the other and rolling from the heel to the toe (this is an arch strengthener). The spotter supports the child's lower arm and wrist. Most children will initially inch their way along the beam by sliding one foot behind the other. Stress *walking*.

2. Ask the youngsters to walk across the beam with no assistance and then to leap off the end. The instructor should watch for foot deformities and weaknesses.
   Note:
   Younger children's foot muscles may not be finely developed. Weaknesses are normal at this age. Try to correct them before they become habits.

3. Have the youngsters walk half-way across the beam, pivot by rising onto the toes and turning half-way around, and return to the beginning of the beam.

4. Have the youngsters walk half-way across the beam and squat, keeping one foot in front of the other with the arms extended to the sides and the back straight. (The young-

Figure 53.
Hands up for balance.

Figure 54. Instructor watches
one child on balance beam while
tying shoe of another.

sters may tend to: (1) lean forward with their buttocks sticking into the air, or (2) perform a half-squat.) After the full squat is completed, ask the children to rise to a standing position and walk to the end of the beam. Make a game of not falling from the beam. This writer tells her students they'll be gobbled up by pretend-alligators if they fall into the water (onto the floor). Some readers may find this statement offensive, but in my experience children are not afraid of these games and they serve to motivate rather than deter.

Sawhorses

Type used: Sawhorses can be purchased in any building-supply house or lumberyard. They are inexpensive, and when brightly painted serve as an excellent balance beam.

Purposes and objectives: Sawhorse work should follow the small balance beam in order of progression. It is higher from the floor, making balance essential. Sawhorses help the child overcome fear of heights and are excellent for the teaching of coordination and balance. The instructor should look for weaknesses in the feet of the students and make corrections as they occur. *Note*: Hard mats must be placed under or around the horses (soft ones will cause them to wobble). Spotting is mandatory.

Sawhorse Activities

The following steps are recommended in sawhorse work:
1. Walk forward, keeping one foot in front of the other, with arms extended to the sides for balance. The spotter should initially hold the wrist and lower arm of the child until he feels secure in his own capabilities. Watch for students inching one foot behind the other. Since the beams are two feet off the floor, the young child will be very apprehensive. Upon reaching the end of the horse, stand in front of the child, hold both of his hands, and help him leap off and down to the floor. Make sure he slightly bends his knees and leans forward when landing.
2. As their confidence develops, ask the children to walk across the horses holding only one finger of the spotter for security rather than balance. Have the children leap from the end with a finger assist.

Figure 55. *Walking across the sawhorse with assistance.*

Figure 56. *Leaping from the end of the sawhorse.*

3. Walk across and leap from the beam with no assistance. The spotter should stand at the child's side with her arms up, near his trunk, in case he loses his balance.

4. Walk half-way across the horse and squat (back straight, one foot in front of the other, knees bent, and arms extended to the sides). Stand, walk, and jump off the horse to the floor.

5. Walk across the horses, pivot, and walk back. The children will need assistance when pivoting because they are not yet able to move on the balls of their feet without losing

balance. It takes tremendous foot and arch strength to perform this successfully.

6. Advanced students may be taught to kneel. When starting, one leg must be pushed back as the hands hold the sides of the horse (fingers underneath, thumbs on top). The most difficult part is going down and coming up from the kneeling position. The spotter should stand to the side of the child and hold one of his elbows; the spotter's other hand is free to catch the performer if he loses his balance.

Spotter

Movement Exploration

Sawhorses can be used for:
    Horses.
    Airplanes.
    Boats.
    Automobiles.
    Trains.

Sawhorses And Plank

Type used: A four-foot by eight-foot piece of plywood is placed across the sawhorses. Any lumberyard stocks these items at a fairly inexpensive price (or ask for donations).

Purposes and objectives: The children will learn three skills that require balance and coordination: climbing, walking, and jumping from a height.

Figure 57. Holding the spotter's hands . . .

Figure 58. . . . the child leans forward, ready to jump.

Figure 59. Ready for takeoff.

Sawhorse And Plank Activities

1. The children line up in single file and climb up the side of the sawhorse by stepping on the brace and lifting one knee at a time to the plank.
2. From the crawling position (in which they reach the top of the plank) they stand and walk across to the end. Most children should be able to accomplish steps *1* and *2* with little assistance (they're already accustomed to heights from sawhorse work).
3. Facing the spotter and holding her hands, each child jumps out and down, leaning forward with the knees bent. The child must have confidence in the spotter. (Notice the fearful expression on the face of the child in figure 57.) Tell him he can do it. Give as much assistance as is required. Make a game by yelling "Geronimo!" as each child jumps.
4. Eventually the children will climb, walk, and jump with no help. Some will be able to do it sooner than others. The children still must learn that their feet should be together. The child in figure 59 has perfected the skills and is in a "ready" position for the takeoff.

Movement Exploration

Sawhorses and planks can be used for a:
Bus.
Bed.
Flying carpet.

Stegel

Type used: The stegel is a piece of apparatus of German design with tremendous potential, if fully utilized. It can be built from thirteen two-inch by four-inch by eight-foot beams. Carefully observe the pictures when constructing it. We hired a carpenter and the cost was $35 for labor and materials. The materials alone ran approximately $20.

Purposes and objectives: Strength, flexibility, balance, agility, and coordination are all developed when performing skills on the stegel. It is a very unusual piece of equipment and the only one needed if the instructor has a limited budget. *Note*: Place the stegel on hard mats or surround it with softer ones. Spotting is mandatory.

Figure 60. The stegel . . .

Figure 61. . . . a versatile piece of apparatus.

Stegel Activities

Climbing

The children may climb individually or in groups. Ask them to walk up the steps (they may use the hands on the wood for support), climb over the top, and down the other side. Each child's approach will be different. Some will step with ease over the top rung while others will need either verbal or physical assistance. The top step may pose a problem since there is nothing higher to grasp and the body weight must be evenly distributed on the same plane.

Figure 62. Climbing the stegel . . .

Figure 63. . . . using hands for support.

Figure 64. Pulling on the stegel.

Pulling

Ask the children to lie on their stomachs, grasping each rung and pulling their legs (dead weight) behind them. This exercise can be performed only by children with strong upper trunk and arm muscles, but all should be encouraged to give it a try.

Movement Exploration

The stegel can be used for a:
Bus (stegel can seat many).
Horse.
Car.
Chariot.

Relay Races (Recommended for children four-and-a-half years and older.)

Teams line up in single file formation behind the stegel. On a given signal each child climbs up and over it. After one child lands on the floor, the next team player continues the same skill. The first group to complete the race and be seated is declared the winner.

Beam Work

1. Ask each child to walk across each rung, one foot in front of the other. The youngsters are spotted in the same manner as in the sawhorse work (see figure 65). They graduate from the lowest beam to the highest. Spotting is essential! The children are four feet off the ground and will be nervous. Have them walk (not inch along) with the entire foot on the beam. Watch for foot weaknesses.
2. Walk with no assistance (see figure 66).
3. Walk, pivot, and return to the starting point, with or without assistance.
4. Walk half-way across the beam, half-squat, stand, and continue walking with assistance. *Note*: Steps 3 and 4 are for children who have advanced skills.

Figure 65.
Walking with assistance . . .

Figure 66.
. . . and alone.

Jumping

Stand on the lowest rung with the back facing the beam. Jump. Gradually work up to the highest beam, jumping from each step along the way. The youngsters jump out and down. When a child reaches the top step, ask him to face one end of the stegel and jump out and down. He will initially want and need a spotter.

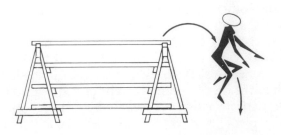

Ladder

Type used: Use a wooden ladder six to eight feet high; these are found in any hardware or discount store. Paint each step a different color.

Purposes and objectives: Use of the ladder teaches the proper techniques for climbing, turning, and jumping that require agility, coordination, and balance. Painting each step a different color educates the children in color awareness when they are asked to climb to the red step or jump from the blue step, for example.

Ladder Activities

Figures 67-71 best illustrate how to instruct and assist in jumping from the ladder. Make sure no one is standing in front of the ladder before the jump is performed. Insist the children jump out and down. Once the children show confidence, mark a line on the floor as a jumping goal.

Movement Exploration

Ladders can be used for a:
Tree.
Car.
Truck.
Mountain.

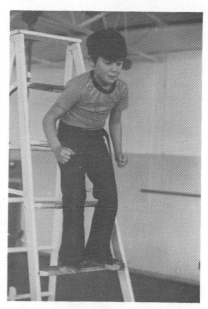

Figure 67.
Jumping with two-handed assist.

Figure 68.
Ready to jump . . .

Figure 69.
. . . arms back and knees bent.

Figure 70.
Knees bent, arms up for balance.

Figure 71. Jumping from fourth step (note that feet are together).

Jungle Gym

Type used: Since our budget was limited, we looked for a plastic or metal jungle gym in a local discount toy store and found one for under $10. If the sky is the limit, one can find very elaborate jungle gyms with removable parts ranging from $50 to $200.

Purposes and objectives: Agility, flexibility, arm and leg strength, and coordination are developed through the use of jungle gyms. They should be stable and have no rough edges or screws that jut out, thus causing injuries. *Note*: Place jungle gyms on hard mats or surround them with softer ones.

Jungle Gym Activities

1. Work with the children individually. Ask each one to climb up the side of the jungle gym and hang from the cross bar by his hands (thumbs go under and around bar meeting the fingers over the bar). Help the youngster drop to the floor since he may be afraid to release his grip. If the jungle gym is short, stand facing the child, holding his wrists. If it is tall, stand beneath the youngster, catching his trunk on the descent to the floor.

 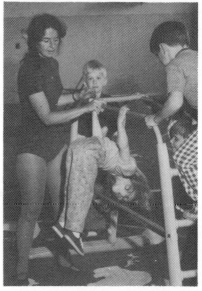

Figure 72. Jungle gym activities with full assistance . . .

Figure 73. . . . partial assistance . . .

Figure 74. . . . and no physical assistance.

2. Ask the child to climb up the side of the jungle gym and stand on the lower cross-rung. Holding the top rung, he should lift one leg at a time over that rung in between his hands (shoulder width apart), with the spotter holding one hand on the child's wrist and the other against his back. Help him to release his grip, enabling his body to hang from the knees. The spotter cradles the youngster's back and places the other arm across the child's feet so they won't slide off the bar.

3. Help the child rise up (by looking at his feet) to a sitting position. He dismounts in the same manner as he got up.
4. *Skin the Cat*: (Recommended for children four-and-a-half years and older)

   Climb and hang from the knees as in step 2. Instead of rising as in step 3, the child grips onto the bar, bringing his feet over his head, releasing the grip, and landing with his feet on the floor. Spotting techniques and performance are shown in figures 72-74.

Movement Exploration

The jungle gym serves as a:
   Bus.
   Horse.
   Skimobile.
   Camel.

Note: More elaborate gyms come equipped with: (1) poles for sliding; (2) ladders for climbing; (3) rings, ropes, and bars for hanging and swinging. Remember the age and ability of the group. Many children will progress faster than others. Everyone should be expected to try everything at least a number of times. Some children will need firmness while others respond best to gentleness or coaxing. Know each child! He is an individual, not one of the herd.

Maze

At the end of each class period, this writer combines most of the apparatus and small equipment into a maze system.

A suggested plan is as follows:

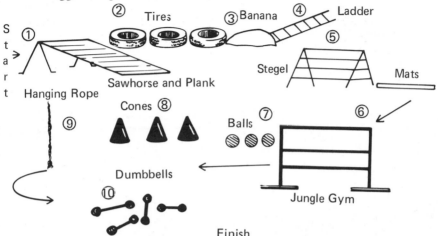

1. Climb the horse and slide down the plank.
2. Walk over the tires, across the banana, and up the ladder.
3. Walk across the stegel and jump to the floor.
4. Climb the jungle gym and do *Skin The Cat.*
5. Pick up a ball and dribble it around the cones.
6. Swing from the rope.
7. Pick up a dumbbell and march to the other side of the room.

Spotters will be needed at the ladder, stegel, jungle gym, and rope. If the instructor is alone she should work individually with the children until they are past the swinging rope.

Children love the maze and make up stories as they go along, pretending to be on safaris, bear hunts, bus rides, and mountainous journeys. The maze serves as a good review in the use of equipment or apparatus, lends itself to movement exploration, and contributes to the development of short term memory.

Chapter 7

Game-Type Activities For The Young Child

Boys and girls throughout the world love games. The history of games began when man first was created and can be seen through pictographs. Games are one of the few areas in which there is a universal language. When given a ball and a stick, most children in any part of the globe will create some type of activity that involves competition and coordination, either with others or alone. Games never lose their luster, whether they be checkers for the over-seventy set or relay races for the first-grader. They serve as a recreational outlet that diversifies the mundane routine of life.

Games present a structure in which children can utilize the basic skills in a challenging and exciting setting. Youngsters should have the opportunity to create simple games. The instructor can set ground rules (equipment, playing area, and number of participants) for the children to work around. For example, the area might cover half of a gymnasium, using two playground balls and ten participants. Let the children create the rest: rules, points, object of the game, teams. Older children (five-and-a-half and older) should be able to think of easy games once they have a basic background in the physical education program.

Three-and-a-half to five-year-old youngsters can have a modi-fied game program. They should not be expected to turn out as professional soccer or volleyball players after a year's work. What *can* be expected is better knowledge of self, application of problem solving, and the development of better coordination. (see chapter 9: *Relay Races*). The teacher initially plays with the group, helping the children to understand the rules and object of each game. By the end of the year, the class should be able to handle familiar games with little assistance.

BENEFITS OF GAMES

Games provide many benefits:
1. Learning to work together and develop strategy;
2. Learning to control movement;
3. Increasing awareness of space limitations;
4. Participation in a structured situation;
5. Fun!

CONDUCTING GAMES

Initially, games should be handled through a systematic approach. Some practical suggestions in conducting them should be considered:
1. Thoroughly explain the game to be played. Talk as briefly as possible and to the point. Ask for questions and clear up the confusing points before proceeding with the game.
2. Place the youngsters in the proper formation such as circle, line, or teams. Specifically call the children's names when seating or dividing the class.
3. If there is a team situation (not until children are four-and-a-half years and older) try to have colored arm bands or removable stickers for each group (for example, team *A* is blue, team *B* is red) to avoid confusion.
4. If a secret number is given to each child, as in the game *Spud*, have him repeat his number to you. He may not have heard what you said and may be too embarrassed to ask to have it repeated.
5. Walk to and point out each boundary line to avoid a mix-up. If a game calls for bases, clearly number each one.
6. State the rules. Make them simple and flexible for preschoolers.

7. Remove all objects lying around that may interfere with the game or cause harm through tripping. Tie all shoes before proceeding with the activity. It seems as if preschoolers constantly have shoes that come off or are untied, so double knot them.

8. Ask the parents to dress their children in practical and comfortable clothing. Most little people are very clothes-conscious and won't want to mess up a new dress or play outfit.

9. It is common for preschoolers to bring favorite toys or stuffed animals to class for security. Suggest that they leave them on a chair to "watch" their "mommies" or "daddies" play.

10. Walk through the entire game a number of times before playing it. Again, ask if there are any questions and specifically call on a youngster who looks puzzled. He may have a valid question that will benefit the entire class, but is too shy to ask the teacher.

11. Play the entire game and help each student having a problem, for example if in *Wonderball* a child receives the ball but holds onto it instead of passing it.

12. Once the children are sure of the game, adhere to the rules. To illustrate: In the game of *Wonderball*, if a child is holding the ball when "Out" is said, he must move out of the circle and watch the rest of the game. Initially, give him a number of chances by saying "OK, the next time we're playing for real." This writer tries to be "out" first and pretends to cry like a baby, much to the glee of the children. They can see how silly it is to make such a fuss about being "out." Remind them that there is always a next time. Alternative approach: Instead of "out" use the word "in." Have children move to the center of the circle if they are eliminated.

13. After they have learned a number of games, ask the class which ones they would like to play. Give one or two children their choice each time the class meets.

14. Since there are so many unfamiliar concepts in every game, teach only one new game per lesson.

15. Give all the children a chance to participate. Don't let the more skilled players dominate the game.

16. The instructor should remember that games should be simple and fun.

17. It should be noted that some of the games are rather complex and may be too difficult for individual children. If this be the case, I suggest that the rules be greatly modified or, if need be, some of the games eliminated. The activities chosen in this guide have proven successful in my experience, but the teacher should use his or her own discretion according to the needs and abilities of each class.

CHART OF ACTIVITIES

The following chart may be helpful for the teacher in choosing a game in which little equipment is needed for a specific age group. *Note:* Small groups should not be less than 4 or 5; large, not more than 20.

ACTIVITY	AGE LEVEL	NUMBER IN GAME	EQUIPMENT NEEDED	TYPE OF GAME
Monster	2 1/2+	unlimited (in pairs)	none	running
Stoop Tag	3	large	none	tag
Follow the Leader	3	large	none	moving
Mother May I	3	no more than 8	none	moving
Poor Kitty	3	no more than 8-10	none	standing
Circus Game	3 1/2+	large	none	running
Color Tag	3 1/2+	large	none	tag
Robot	3+	large	none	basic movement patterns
Simon Says	3 1/2+	large	none	moving
Huckle, Buckle, Bean Stalk	3 1/2+	unlimited	eraser	hide & seek
Freeze	3 1/2+	unlimited (in pairs)	none	running
Magic Carpet	3 1/2+	unlimited	marked floor	running
Red Light	3 1/2+	large	none	moving
Hunter	4+	large	none	running
Back to Back	4+	large (in pairs)	none	running

Duck, Duck, Goose	4+	no more than 15 per circle	none	running
Dog and Bone	4+	large	none	sitting
Arf-Arf	4+	large	none	sitting
Birds Fly	4+	large	none	sitting
Man from Mars	4+	large	none	running
What Time Is It, Mr. Fox?	4+	large	none	running
Grandma's Basket	4+	no more than 8 per circle	none	sitting quietly
Monkey in the Middle	4+	unlimited (in 3's)	playground balls	throwing & catching
Shadow	4+	unlimited (in pairs)	none	any type of movement
Telephone	4 1/2+	unlimited	none	sitting quietly
Call Ball	5+	8-10 in each circle	playground ball	running
Spud	5+	no more than 10	playground ball	running
I Say Stoop	5+	large (in pairs)	none	standing
Farm Animals	5+	large (in pairs)	none	hide & seek
Cat & Dog	5+	no more than 10 in circle	none	running
Steal the Bacon	5+	no more than 12	eraser	running
Line Soccer	5+	no more than 12	playground ball	running
Kickball	5+	large	playground ball	running
Punchball	5+	large	playground or beach ball	running
Statues	5	no more than 10	none	moving/freeze

DESCRIPTION OF GAMES

Note:

Each game lists a recommended age level at which to *introduce* the activity in the child's life. All of the games may be played by children six, seven, and eight years of age. For instance, this writer has used Steal the Bacon and Kickball for third grade classes with positive results.

Monster

Level: Two-and-a-half years and older.
Purpose: Overcoming fears.
Equipment needed: None.
Location: Any large area.
Organization: Have the class pair off and hold hands with their partners. Give the children an imaginary box of popcorn and tiptoe around the gym looking for big, green monsters. Pretend to see one and stop, holding up the box of corn for the friendly monster to eat. Ask the children if they see him (most will; the younger ones initially will be confused but will later join in on the fun). Tell them he's going to stand up and they'd all better move out of his way. Partners should run as quickly as possible to the opposite side of the room.
Variations: Make a game out of anything that is fearful to the child. Pretend that you're walking in the dark and make it pleasant by asking the children to see a sleeping deer or frog. Try to cover as much space as possible with variations of basic movements (as in *Follow The Leader*).
Things to watch for: The children are in pairs for security. They feel more confident holding someone's hand when exploring the unknown. It is the instructor's creative mind that can make this game imaginative and enjoyable.

• Stoop Tag

Level: Three years and older.
Purpose: Change of direction; large muscle movement.
Equipment needed: None.
Location: Gymnasium, playroom, or playground.
Organization: The players stand anywhere in the playing area. One child is *It*. He must try to tag a child before she or

he stoops to the ground. If he does tag someone, that person becomes the next *It*.

Things to watch for: The children must lightly tap each other, not push or shove.

Follow The Leader

Level: Three years and older.
Purpose: Following directions; motor learning.
Equipment needed: None.
Location: Any play area with boundary lines.
Organization: The class stands facing a chosen leader. Everything he does, the class must follow. It may vary from hopping to jumping or include any variety of movements. Give a number of children the chance to be the leader.

Things to watch for: This is an excellent activity to use with rhythms. The children may face or follow behind the leader. The teacher should demonstrate the game first.

Mother, May I?

Level: Three years and older.
Purpose: Listening to and following directions.
Equipment needed: None.
Location: Playroom or playground.
Organization: The children line up with their backs against a wall. They face the person chosen to be the *Mother* standing approximately twenty-five feet away. She or he names a child and tells him what activity he must perform. The child must ask "May I?" The *Mother* says *yes* and the child proceeds to do what was commanded. If the child doesn't ask "May I?" he or she must go back to the starting line. The object is to tag *Mother* and take her place. Sample dialogue: *Mother*: Charlie, you may take ten giant steps. *Charlie*: May I? *Mother*: Yes, you may. Possible steps are baby step, scissor steps (jump and cross feet), giant steps, crab walk, umbrella step (twirl while doing each step), hops, jumps, etc.

Things to watch for: The two-and-a-half to three-and-a-half-year-olds will have trouble remembering to ask "May I?" The teacher should say it with him until he can do it independently.

Poor Kitty

Level: Three years and older.
Purpose: Self-control.
Equipment needed: None.
Location: Playground or playroom.
Organization: The children form a circle with hands at their sides. One child is chosen as *Kitty* and kneels in the center of the circle. *Kitty* must crawl to any child and meow, trying to make him laugh. He must pat *Kitty* on the head, looking at him and saying "Poor Kitty." The "Meow" and "Poor Kitty" are repeated three times in all. If the child doing the patting laughs, he is the next *Kitty*. If he doesn't laugh, *Kitty* must move onto another player.
Things to watch for: Encourage the *Kitty* to make funny meows and to look directly at the "patter." It is amazing to see how serious the youngsters can be at this age.

Circus Game

Level: Three-and-a-half years and older.
Purpose: Developing the imagination.
Equipment needed: None.
Location: Playground or playroom.
Organization: One child is the *Circus Master* and stands in the center of the circle formed by the other children. He pretends to have a whip and commands the children to walk like various circus animals (i.e., "Tigers ready? Good! Walk forward."). When he wishes, the *Circus Master* calls "Stop!" He takes his place in the circle, and another child comes forward to the center.
Things to watch for: A pre-arranged order for *Circus Masters* can be established. It allows the children to think of an animal before it is their turn.

Color Tag

Level: Three-and-a-half-years and older.
Purpose: Change of level; change of direction; learning color concepts.
Equipment needed: None.
Location: Playground or gymnasium.

Figure 75. Robot.

Organization: One child is chosen to be *It*. He must run after the class and try to tag them. They are "safe" if they stoop down and name a color before they are tagged. The first child tagged is *It*.

Things to watch for: Set specific boundary lines. Don't allow children to stay in a stooped position. They must start moving immediately after naming a color. Review colors by pointing to the children's clothing (i.e., "What color shirt is Billy wearing? Suzy, what color is your belt?").

Robot

Level: Three years and older.

Purpose: Following directions; body and spatial awareness.

Equipment needed: None.

Location: Playroom or playground.

Organization: The children are told they are "robots." The instructor, in a mechanical tone of voice (as if she were a robot too) tells the children to *walk forward; walk backward; kneel; roll over, become rusty,* or any number of ideas that may range from simple to complex. Instruct the children that they cannot bump into another child while performing any of the movements.

Things to watch for: Relatively little can go wrong (unless the children bump into each other). This is a very enjoyable activity both for the children and the teacher.

Simon Says

Level: Three-and-a-half years and older.
Purpose: Following directions; perceptual-conceptual learning.
Equipment needed: None.
Location: Playground or playroom.
Organization: The youngsters stand in front of a pre-chosen *Simon*. Whatever "Simon says" the children must do. If the term "Simon says" doesn't come before the command, the children should not perform it. If they do, they are out. The last child left in the game is the next *Simon* (i.e., "Simon says jump up and down. Simon says kneel." Children should do as indicated. "Stand up." Children should not stand up, but stay in a kneeling position.).
Things to watch for: Simon Says is a more complex form of *Follow The Leader*. Have a number of trial games first. The instructor should be the initial *Simon* for demonstration purposes. Give the children a number of chances before being "out." If the game is too difficult eliminate children being "out" and simply use as a direction-following game.

Huckle, Buckle, Beanstalk

Level: Three-and-a-half years and older.
Purpose: Observation and self-discipline; spatial awareness.
Equipment needed: Small object (eraser, book).
Location: Playroom.
Organization: Some small object is hidden by the teacher while the players are outside the room. They are called in to hunt for it. Anyone seeing the object walks to the teacher (who is in the center of the room) and calls "Huckle, buckle, beanstalk." The first child to spot the object is the next person to hide it.
Note: The "hider" should tell the children they are getting warm (close to the object), cold (far away from the object), and hot (next to the object).
Things to watch for: Hide the object in plain sight and set limits where it can be hidden (not inside desks or in closets). Make sure the children don't peek into the room. Show the object before hiding it (they can't search for it if they don't know what they're looking for).

Freeze

Level: Three-and-a-half years and older.

Purpose: Following directions; change of direction; body and spatial awareness.

Equipment needed: None.

Location: Playground or gymnasium.

Organization: The children pair off. The instructor says "Run away from your partners." They must run in a different direction from their partner. On the given command of "Freeze," the children must immediately stop. After the room is quiet and all the players are frozen, the instructor yells "Find your partners!" The children must run to their partners, squat down, and hold each other's hands. The last pair is eliminated and become "judges" with the teacher.

Things to watch for: Freeze is a marvelous game to play at the end of every class. Insist the children run far apart. If there is a tie, repeat the game until there is a winner.

Magic Carpet

Level: Three-and-a-half years and older.

Purpose: Large muscle development; following commands; body and spatial awareness.

Equipment needed: Four *Magic Carpets* (marked areas approximately five feet by five feet) in a circular arrangement around the playroom.

Location: Playroom or outdoors.

Organization: Select one child to be the leader. The rest of the children follow the leader as he runs or skips across the *Magic Carpets*. At the signal from the teacher ("Freeze!"), all players come to an immediate halt. Those who stop on a *Magic Carpet* get a point. This is repeated a number of times. The player with the lowest number of points at the end of the game is the winner.

Things to watch for: The teacher should write down the children's names and the points received. Have the players halt immediately.

Red Light

Level: Three-and-a-half years and older.

Purpose: Change of speed and coordination.
Equipment needed: None.
Location: Playground or gymnasium.
Organization: The player selected to be *It* stand on a goal line marked across one end of the play area. The other players stand at the starting line at the opposite end of the room. The child who is *It* turns his back to the players and calls "One-two-three-Red Light!" The players run toward the goal line, but most stop on the word "Red Light!" On this signal, *It* turns to face the players. If he sees anyone moving his feet, the player is sent back to the starting line. The first one to tag *It* is the next *It*.
Things to watch for: Make sure *It* says "One-two-three-Red Light" loudly enough to be heard and doesn't turn around before saying "Red Light."

Hunter

Level: Four years and older.
Purpose: Following directions; large muscle movement; motor development.
Equipment needed: None.
Location: Outdoors or playroom. Mark off a long goal line and set boundaries for the game.
Organization: One child is selected to be the hunter. He stands in front of the class and asks "Who wants to go hunting with me?" The children respond, "I do!" They form a single line behind the hunter and follow him wherever he chooses to go, doing everything he does. Suddenly, he calls "Bang!" The children must run past the goal. The first player over the line is the next hunter.
Things to watch for: Have the hunter walk as far away from the goal line as possible before saying "Bang!"

Back To Back

Level: Four years and older.
Purpose: Quick response to directions; motor development.
Equipment needed: None.
Location: Outdoors or playroom.
Organization: There should be an uneven number of children. On a given signal, each child stands back to back (hooking elbows) with another player. One child is without a partner. On

the next signal, all children change partners with the extra player seeking a partner.

Things to watch for: Don't let the children run back to the same partner. Give a variety of commands such as "Change partners leaping like a frog," or "Change partners, crawling like a snake," to make the game more interesting.

Duck, Duck, Goose

Level: Four years and older.

Purpose: Instantaneous reaction; change of level.

Equipment needed: None.

Location: Outdoors or playroom.

Organization: Children kneel in a circle formation. A chosen runner runs around the circle tapping each child lightly on the head and saying "Duck." When he wishes, he changes the word to "Goose"; that child quickly rises, chasing him around the circle back to his vacant place. If the runner gets back safely, the chaser is the new runner. If the runner is tagged, he must sit in the middle of the circle (the *Duck Pond*).

Variation: Have the children use words that go together in place of "Duck" and "Goose," i.e., "peanut butter and jelly"; "socks and shoes"; "red and green"; or "top and bottom."

Things to watch for: It is important for the players to be in a half-kneeling position. It takes too long to stand from a cross-legged position. Have the players choose a *Goose* quickly to avoid a long, drawn-out game.

Dog And Bone

Level: Four years and older.

Purpose: Developing the sense of hearing; problem solving.

Equipment needed: Bone (or any object that is easily picked up).

Location: Playroom or outdoors.

Organization: One child is selected to be the *Dog*. He sits with his back to the class (also seated) and covers his eyes. The *Dog's Bone* is placed near his back. A child selected by the teacher attempts to sneak up on the *Dog* and steal the bone without being heard. If the *Dog* hears someone coming, he says "Bow wow." The child who successfully takes the bone without being heard is the next *Dog*.

Things to watch for: The entire class should be very quiet and no hints should be given by the seated children. The instructor should stand in front of the *Dog* (to make sure he doesn't peek). It takes much self-control for the four-year-old not to peek.

Arf-Arf

Level: Four years and older.
Purpose: Developing the sense of hearing.
Equipment needed: Any small object that will serve as a bone.
Location: Playroom or outdoors.
Organization: One child is chosen to be the *Dog*. He sits with his back to the class and covers his eyes. A player is selected by the teacher to quietly retrieve the bone placed in back of the *Dog*. The child disguises his voice and says "Arf arf," returning to his seat with the bone. All the children put their hands behind their backs and look forward. The *Dog* must then turn around and has two chances to guess the culprit. If he properly guesses, he has another turn as the *Dog*; if he doesn't, the culprit becomes the new *Dog*.
Things to watch for: The children should look forward, not at the culprit.

Birds Fly

Level: Four years and older.
Purpose: A "thinking" game, probably one of the first for four-year-olds. Problem solving; perceptual awareness.
Equipment needed: None.
Location: Outdoors or playroom.
Organization: The player chosen as *It* stands in front of the class and says, "Ducks fly, horses fly, birds fly," etc. When he names an animal that *does* fly, the class should wave their arms up and down. When he names an animal that doesn't fly, they must not "fly." (*It* always does the flying motion to confuse the players.) Any child who "flies" when he shouldn't is eliminated. The last child becomes the new *It*.
Things to watch for: The instructor should discuss which animals fly and which ones don't before playing.

Man From Mars

Level: Four years and older.
Purpose: Learning color concepts.
Equipment needed: None.
Location: Gymnasium or outdoors.
Organization: Starting and goal lines approximately thirty feet apart should be marked. The children stand on the starting line facing a youngster who is the *Man From Mars* and stands on a spot ten feet from the group. The players ask, "Man from Mars, may I chase you to the stars?" He replies, "Yes, if you're wearing the color_____" (names a color). If they are wearing the color he names, they must chase him and try to tag him. The first person to do so, becomes the next *Man*.
Variation: *Red Rover*. "Red Rover, Red Rover, if you have on blue come over." Tagged children help tag group until there is one child left untagged, who is the next *Red Rover*.

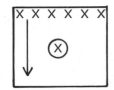
Children must run to the other side of the room without being tagged.

Caller "Red Rover"

Things to watch for: Review the colors with the children. Observe their outfits and ask the colors they are wearing.

What Time Is It, Mr. Fox?

Level: Four years and older.
Purpose: Learning numbers from one to twelve; learning time concepts.
Equipment needed: None.
Location: Playroom or outdoors.
Organization: Mark off a starting line and a standing spot for *Mr. Fox* thirty feet apart. The children stand on the starting line, facing a child chosen as *Mr. Fox*.
Children: What time is it, Mr. Fox?
Fox: One o'clock. (Children move forward one time.)
Children: What time is it, Mr. Fox?
Fox: Six o'clock. (Children move forward six times.)
Children: What time is it Mr. Fox?

Fox: Midnight! (Children turn around and run back to starting line.)

Each time a number is stated, the children step forward that many times, getting closer and closer to *Mr. Fox*. When he says "Midnight!" they must run back to the starting line, trying not to be tagged by him. The first child tagged becomes the new *Mr. Fox*.

Things to watch for: Count from one to twelve with the children. Demonstrate the game. Make sure when they are *Mr. Fox* they don't say every number from one to twelve. (It will become boring unless it is done rapidly.)

Grandma's Basket

Level: Four years and older.
Purpose: Memory testing.
Equipment needed: None.
Location: Playroom or outdoors.
Organization: Children sit in a circle (no more than eight per circle). The first player starts by saying, "I pack my Grandma's basket with_____" (apple, banana, car, etc.—he names anything). The second player repeats what the first person said and adds a new item. This continues around the circle. Each child must repeat what all the others have said before adding his item. If one child forgets the items, the game starts over and he is the new leader.

Things to watch for: It is helpful for the children to remember what each player has said (i.e., Susie said "Apple"; Billy said "Tomato"). This is an excellent game for automobile trips and can be played by the entire family. It also aids in developing short-term memory.

Monkey In The Middle

Level: Four years and older.
Purpose: Agility and eye-hand coordination.
Equipment needed: One playground ball per three players.
Location: Flat surface.
Organization: The class is divided into groups of three. Two children face each other approximately ten feet apart. The third child is the *Monkey* and stands in between the partners. They attempt to throw or roll the ball around or over the *Monkey*.

The *Monkey* tries to intercept the ball. If he does, he becomes a thrower and the child who accidentally threw the ball to the *Monkey*, becomes the new *Monkey*.

Things to watch for: The youngsters should know how to handle a ball with ease before attempting the game. In order to avoid conflict, have the first player to touch the ball be the one to keep it (i.e., *Monkey* and thrower have a tug of war over the ball, but the *Monkey* touched it first).

Shadow (Mirror Image)

Level: Four years and older.
Purpose: Exact miming of a partner; spatial awareness.
Equipment needed: None.
Location: Outdoors or playroom.

Figure 76.
The shadows . . .

Figure 77.
. . . mime
actions exactly.

Organization: The class is divided into pairs. One child is *It* and faces his partner or "shadow." The shadow must follow everything *It* does (i.e., making funny faces, jumping, hopping, singing, running, etc.). After a given time, they change roles.

Things to watch for: This is an excellent game for developing a keen sense of observation. It is much more difficult to perform than it sounds. Once the children are good at miming, have *It* try to trick the "shadow" by suddenly sitting down and standing up or clapping three times and kneeling (any unexpected movement will do).

Telephone

Level: Four-and-a-half years and older.
Purpose: Developing the sense of hearing.
Equipment needed: None.
Location: Outdoors or playroom.
Organization: The children sit in circle formation. The leader (appointed by the teacher) whispers a statement to the player on his left. He, in turn, whispers what he heard to the next player and so on until it reaches the last child. The last child must tell everyone what he heard, followed by the leader, who tells what was really said. It is extremely amusing to see how "news" changes as it is spread. Choose a new leader each time the game is repeated.

Things to watch for: Ask the children to whisper (not shout into someone's ear) simple statements.

Call Ball

Level: Five years and older.
Purpose: Eye-hand coordination.
Equipment needed: Large playground ball.
Location: Outdoors or playroom.
Organization: The children form a circle around one player who is holding the ball. He throws it into the air and calls a player's name. That child runs forward and tries to catch the ball after one bounce. If successful, he becomes the center player. If not, the center player throws again.

Variation: Have the children catch the ball before it bounces.

Things to watch for: The ball should remain inside the circle (toss the ball up, not forward). Make sure the children know each other's names before playing. *Note*: *Call Ball* should be taught before *Spud*.

Spud

Level: Five years and older (if child is a mature five, this game can be considered).

Purpose: Following a series of directions; memory testing; development of eye-hand coordination.

Equipment needed: Playground ball or beach ball.

Location: Playroom or outdoors.

Organization: The children are each given a secret number by the teacher or "number giver." One child tosses the ball into the air and calls a number (the teacher tells the class the range of numbers, i.e., one through ten). The child with the corresponding number catches the ball and yells "Spud!" Meanwhile, everyone else has run away from the ball but must freeze when "Spud!" is yelled. The child with the ball takes three giant steps and tries to hit the player closest by (below the waist). If the child aimed at is hit, he gets the letter *S* (object: spell out the word *Spud*). If he is missed, the thrower gets an *S*. Everyone comes back to the center of the room. The player who was hit tosses the ball into the air and yells a new number. The first child to be hit (or to miss as thrower) four times, thus spelling out the word *Spud*, goes through the "spanking machine." A spanking machine is formed by the players standing in a single file with their legs apart. The *Spud* child must crawl under their legs and be gently spanked by each of the players.

Things to watch for: Have the children repeat their numbers to you. Walk through the game before playing it. Ask for questions. Insist on gentle taps when spanking the *Spud* child.

I Say Stoop

Level: Five years and older.

Purpose: Develop a keen sense of observation; problem solving; perceptual-conceptual learning.

Equipment needed: None.

Location: Playroom or outdoors.

Organization: The players stand facing a leader chosen by the teacher. The leader gives the command, "I say stoop!" or "I say stand!" The players follow the leader's commands, not his actions. He may stoop (semi-knee bend position) when he says "Stand" or vice versa. The first player who misses becomes the next leader.

Things to watch for: This game may also be played by eliminating the players who miss and having the winner become the leader. Often children will deliberately miss so they can lead the group.

Farm Animals

Level: Five years and older.

Purpose: Balance; developing the sense of hearing and concentration; body and spatial awareness.

Equipment needed: None.

Location: A quiet room.

Organization: The children pair off or form teams of three or four. Each group decides what animal noise they will make. One child in every group is the "animal." The rest of the children stand in the center of the room and shut their eyes. The "animals" go to different corners and make their sound (i.e., *moo, oink, baa*). The children must try to find their animal (eyes still shut). The first group standing together is the winner.

Things to watch for: The instructor should visit each group, insuring no duplication of sounds. Tell the children to keep their arms outstretched when searching for their "animal" to avoid bumping into the other players.

Cat & Dog

Level: Five years and older.

Purpose: Instantaneous decision making; problem solving; development of large muscles.

Equipment needed: None.

Location: Outdoors or playroom.

Organization: Children form a circle and hold hands. One child stands in the center of the circle and is the *Dog*. Another child stands outside the circle and is the *Cat*. On a given signal, the *Dog* must try to tag the *Cat*. They may only enter or leave the circle if the players' arms are up (hands held together forming an arch). If the players leave their arms down, the *Cat* or *Dog* must try another section of the circle and attempt to escape or capture each other. After the *Dog* tags the *Cat*, they switch roles or give their positions to two new children.

Things to watch for: It is very interesting to note how the players approach a blockade. Some are totally confused; others instantly adjust to the situation and try a different line of reason.

Steal The Bacon

Level: Five years and older. (Teacher should use discretion on this game: some five-years-olds will not be able to handle something this complicated.)

Purpose: Develops one on one competition; number concepts.

Equipment needed: Any object that is easy to pick up to serve as the *Bacon*.

Location: Playground or playroom.

Organization: The class is divided into two teams. Each child is given a number (both teams will have the same numbers). The teams face each other on opposite sides of a room behind goal lines, with the *Bacon* (eraser, frisbee) between them. The instructor calls out a number. The child with that number from each team runs to the *Bacon* and tries to steal it back to his own team without being tagged by the opposite team member with the same number. If he makes it, his team is awarded a point. If he is tagged, no team gets the point. The first team to obtain five points is the winner.

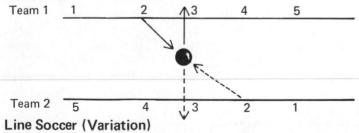

Line Soccer (Variation)

This game is played in the same manner but the *Bacon* is a ball. It may be kicked or thrown to teammates. One or more numbers may be called at the same time.

Things to watch for: If more than one number is called, have the teammates work together and develop strategy (i.e., number one passes the ball to number three, who throws it to his team). Children love these games because of the team work and competition involved.

Kickball

Level: Five years and older. (This game should be modified by eliminating some of the rules for the five-year-old. It is primarily taught for eye-and-foot coordination, and is an early form of competition.)

Purpose: Eye-hand coordination; teamwork; competition; large muscle development.

Equipment needed: Playground or soccer ball.

Location: Outdoors or playroom with four marked bases each twenty to thirty feet apart in a rectangular or diamond formation.

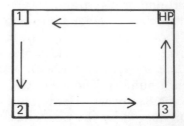

Organization: The class is divided into two equal teams. One is in the field, the other is "up" behind home plate. The team in the field should take various positions covering first, second, and third base; catcher; shortstop; pitcher; and right, center, and left fields. If the teams are small (four or five players), have the players take strategic positions (first and third bases, pitcher, shortstop, and catcher).

The pitcher rolls the ball to an opposite team member standing in front of home plate. He must kick the ball and run to first base without being tagged.

1. If a fly ball is caught, the player is out.
2. A player making four foul balls is out.
3. The team that is up at home plate must make two outs before going to the field.
4. Have the first team with five runs win. As they mature, have five innings.
5. A home run constitutes getting all the way around the three bases and back to home plate.

6. A child is not out unless tagged by the ball in the hands of a player. (It may not be rolled, which could cause tripping).

Punchball (Variation)

Punchball is played with the same rules as *Kickball* except that the player must punch the ball with one hand while supporting it with the other. He may hit it with an open palm, with the knuckles, with the top of a closed fist, in an underhand method, overhand style, or side arm swing. All of these points will have to be carefully explained, demonstrated, and attempted before playing the game.

Things to watch for: Teach kicking or punching a ball before attempting the game. Go over all the rules, bases, and responsibilities of the players before playing. Make sure there are no questions. Play one inning for demonstration purposes. It will take an entire class period to first teach *Kickball*. Have patience. The entire team concept will be unfamiliar for many of the children.

Statues

Level: Five years and older.
Purpose: Balance and imagination.
Equipment needed: None.
Location: Playroom or outdoors (preferably on a soft surface).
Organization: One child is chosen as the "turner" and picks a category for the class (bathing beauties, funniest, ugliest). The turner spins each child around. (The turner holds an extended arm of the player and swings him around, letting go after one spin). The child must freeze the way he lands and look silly, funny, or ugly (according to the chosen category). The turner judges the *Statues*. The best one wins and is the new turner.

Things to watch for: The turner shouldn't jerk the players when spinning them. If a problem does arise, the instructor should do the spinning while the last winner judges the *Statues*.

Chapter 8

Stunt Activities

Stunt activities play an important part in the daily lives of young children. They love to hang, climb, fall, balance, roll, and imitate various characters and objects. It requires great courage and daring to place oneself in a suspended position in mid-air or rely on a partner for balance. Trust is an important concept that children must learn when performing stunts. Movement exploration incorporates many of the stunts, such as *Bear Walk, Lame Dog Walk, Crab Walk*, and *Rooster Hop*. It should be noted that tumbling skills are different from stunts. Stunts require agility, coordination, and balance, yet are fairly simple to perform (examples are *Heel Click, Dog Walk*, and *Seal Crawl*); tumbling activities are more difficult and require practice, individual spotting, and the use of mats (examples are *Rolls, Head Stand*, and *Fish Flop*).

Sufficient time should be allowed for practice so that each activity is done well before one proceeds to the next. This kind of activity requires much individual instruction, and spotting techniques are essential to a sound program. The spotter acts as an assistant to the performer by standing close by and guiding him through an activity. Initially the spotter (teacher) will have to physically aid the youngster. For example, for the *Forward*

Roll (somersault) the teacher places one hand behind the child's neck and the other hand under his thighs to help lift the rear end when tumbling. Once the child has tried tumbling, he will need little assistance.

Many stunts should be performed on mats, mattresses, lounge chair pads, or soft grass. Safety is a most important factor. Children with glasses should have them removed or taped, or should wear safety goggles. Pockets should be emptied of their contents. Rubber-soled shoes and proper clothing should be worn. (Girls should wear slacks or culottes.)

Some books state that overweight children should not be forced to perform. This writer feels that all children should participate in the program. It is the instructor's job to positively "psych" the children and to assume they will like stunts and tumbling. Apprehensive children need much attention and have to gain self-confidence. There is nothing more rewarding to a child or the teacher than to achieve success after having initial fear of a stunt. Once he has conquered the fear, he'll attempt almost anything. A child must have faith in the teacher, as she must have faith in the student. At the age of two-and-a-half, most children have less apprehension than older youngsters. They are a joy to work with and the benefits far outweigh the problems.

The lesson plan for a class in stunts and tumbling stunts should consider the following points:

1. Provide warm-up activity to stretch and limber the body.
2. Make sure each child can see the performer (teacher or student) who will demonstrate the stunt.
3. Discuss each stunt. Is it like an animal they can think of? Why is it called, for example, *Donkey Kick*?
4. Have all children perform the skill (including starting position, execution, and finishing position). Work with each one individually.
5. Evaluate progress and repeat the stunt until it is down pat (remembering individual differences).
6. Plan the skills in order of progression, going from the simplest to the more complex.
7. Remember the age of the youngsters. Have the older (or more advanced) children help the younger ones. It gives them a feeling of responsibility and of empathy (understanding the feelings of another individual). It can help serve to eliminate their own fears.

8. Ask for a volunteer parent to help when teaching stunts. Show her how to spot and what is involved in performing the skill.

FORMATION FOR TEACHING STUNTS

The arrangement of the children will depend upon the selected stunts.

Line Formation

The line formation is useful for teaching stunts using a forward motion. There should be a spotter at each mat.

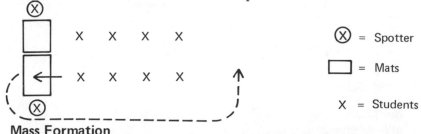

Mass Formation

In this formation, the youngsters are scattered throughout the floor or area. This pattern is useful when all the children are active at one time and need little space, as for example in *Donkey Kick* and *Frog Jump*.

ACTIVITIES FOR THE EARLY CHILDHOOD PROGRAM

Individual Stunts

Bear Walk
Puppy Dog Run
Lame Dog Walk
Elephant Walk
Tight Rope Walk

Gorilla Walk
Duck Walk
Log Roll
Snake Crawl
Frog Legs
Seal Crawl
Donkey Kick
Crab Walk
Heel Click
Heel Slap
Caterpillar Walk
V-Sit
Bridge
Squat Thrust
Rooster Hop
Coffee Grinder

Partner Stunts

Seesaw
Wheelbarrow
Chinese Get-Up
Wring The Towel
Leap Frog

Individual Tumbling Stunts

Forward Roll
Backward Roll
Shoulder Roll
Tripod (Tip-Up)
Modified Cartwheel
Head Stand
Variations Of Backward Roll
Variations Of Forward Roll
Fish Flop

Partner Tumbling Stunts

Angel Stand
Box Stand
Horizontal Stand

Double Forward Roll
Pyramids

It is also good to use stunts in movement exploration. Try to have the stunts develop and encourage creativity. It will make them more fun to perform. An example might be as follows (act out italicized words):

One day Billy decided to visit the zoo. There were all sorts of animals to see in big cages. The *wolf* was *sleeping* but the *big bear* slowly *walked* over to the icy pool and *jumped* in.

Much to the bear's surprise, a *seal* was *clapping* for a *fish* right next to him. Along came a *frog, leaping* after a *fly*, who *swam* in the pool too. Mr. *Snake* joined them and they all *swam* together.

As they looked up they saw a *caterpillar inching* his way along a leaf right over the *elephant* cage. Billy *fed* the elephant some peanuts.

A *gorilla* was *eating* a banana and *walked* up to Billy looking for another handout. The *lioness* was *playing* with an empty box and her *cubs* were *rolling* like *logs* in a corner.

Billy was hungry now and decided to go home and eat lunch. He had had a lovely day at the zoo and would come back tomorrow.

DESCRIPTION OF STUNTS

Note:

Age level in all stunts and tumbling activities is the suggested age at which to introduce the skill. Here again, as with exercises, games, and songs, there is no *end* limit to activities.

Individual Stunts

Bear Walk

Level: Two-and-a-half years and older.
Purpose: Developing arm strength; stretching hamstring muscles (in back of legs).

Description: Bend forward, keep the knees straight, and place the hands on the floor twelve inches in front of the feet. If possible, place the palms on the floor. Walk forward.

Things to watch for: Knees should not be bent when walking forward.

Puppy Dog Run

Level: Two-and-a-half years and older.

Purpose: Balance; hamstring stretch.

Description: Bend forward and place the hands on the floor about two feet in front of the feet. Walk or run forward on all fours.

Things to watch for: Usually the *Puppy Dog Run* poses no problems.

Lame Dog Walk

Level: Two-and-a-half years and older.

Purpose: Coordination and balance.

Figure 78.
The Puppy Dog Run.

Description: Bend forward and place the hands two feet in front of *one* foot. The other foot is raised into the air.

Things to watch for: As the raised leg gets tired, the children may drop it to the floor. Have them alternate "lame leg." Make sure they look up when walking forward.

Elephant Walk

Level: Two-and-a-half years and older.

Purpose: Balance.

Description: Children bend slightly forward, clasping their hands ("trunk") together in front of their tummies. They walk stiff-legged and sway the "trunk" and head.

Figure 79. In the Elephant Walk . . .

Figure 80. . . . the elephants swing their "trunks."

Things to watch for: Legs remain stiff to allow body to roll from side to side. Children may add elephant noises and can pretend to eat peanuts and drink water.

Tight Rope Walk

Level: Two-and-a-half years and older.
Purpose: Balance.
Description: Children walk on a drawn or imaginary line, one foot in front of the other with arms extended to their sides. Tell them they cannot fall from the "rope" because it's a drop of fifty feet into a pool of water.
Things to watch for: The younger the child, the more difficult it will be for him to place his feet one in front of the other. The *Tight Rope Walk* is excellent for developing balance.

Gorilla Walk

Level: Two-and-a-half years and older.
Purpose: Balance.
Description: Bend knees slightly and carry the trunk forward. Arms hang at the sides. As the child walks forward, he should touch the fingers to the ground on each step.
Things to watch for: Children should bend forward enough to allow hands to touch the ground. They can beat their chests and jump around to add a little fun to the stunt.

Duck Walk

Level: Two-and-a-half years and older.

Purpose: Balance and coordination.

Description: The children bend their knees slightly and put hands on the hips with elbows out to the sides. They walk forward in a semi-crouched position and move elbows back and forth while "quacking."

Things to watch for: Have the youngsters lift the knees and move rhythmically from side to side.

Log Roll

Level: Two-and-a-half years and older.

Purpose: Coordination.

Description: Lie on the back with the arms extended over the head and roll to the side. Try to roll in a straight line. It should be performed on a mat.

Things to watch for: The children have a tendency to curl up. Make sure the arms remain over the head and the legs are straight.

Snake Crawl

Level: Two-and-a-half years and older.

Purpose: Developing the imagination and the shoulder muscles.

Description: Lie on the tummy with the weight on the elbows and lower arms. Crawl forward on the elbows, drag the legs, and hiss like a snake. Curl up and lunge forward as if catching a frog.

Things to watch for: Have the legs drag. The *Snake Crawl* usually poses no problems.

Frog Leap

Level: Three years and older.

Purpose: Developing thigh muscles, especially when springing after the flies.

Description: Slightly bend the knees and place the hands on the floor with the arms in between the knees. Move forward by placing the hands a few feet forward and then bringing the feet up to the hands again.

Variation: The children can make sounds of "ribbit, ribbit." Expand the hop by having them sit on imaginary lily pads and leap after flies, gobbling them up.

Things to watch for: Hands may go to the children's sides rather than remain between the knees. Show a picture of a sitting frog.

Seal Crawl

Level: Three years and older.

Purpose: Developing balance and arm strength.

Description: Assume a front-leaning support position (body supported by the hands and feet, back straight) and walk forward with the hands dragging the feet.

Things to watch for: The feet must be dragging with the toes extended backwards. Have the children bark like a seal, roll over and clap for a fish. The *Seal Crawl* takes tremendous arm strength.

Donkey Kick

Figure 81.
The Donkey Kick.

Level: Three years and older.

Purpose: Arm strength and balance.

Description: The child bends at the waist and places his hands on the floor. He kicks both legs into the air and looks up.

Things to watch for: Have arms lock in place to prevent a child from falling onto his nose. Have them "Hee-haw" as they kick.

Crab Walk

Level: Three-and-a-half years and older.

Purpose: Developing arm and leg strength and coordination.

Description: The child squats down and reaches back, putting both hands on the floor without sitting down. The tummy is facing upward. Walk forward, backward, or to the side.

Things to watch for: Children have a tendency to drop the hips. See that the body is kept in a straight line.

Heel Click

Level: Three-and-a-half years and older.

Purpose: Balance and coordination.

Description: Stand with feet slightly apart. Jump up and click heels coming down to the original position.

Things to watch for: The children must get a good spring to have adequate time to click their heels. Have them try it to either side.

Heel Slap

Level: Three-and-a-half years and older.
Purpose: Coordination and balance.
Description: From a standing position, jump into the air and slap the heels with both hands.
Things to watch for: Make sure the children jump up rather than forward.

Caterpillar Walk

Level: Three-and-a-half years and older.
Purpose: Arm strength and hamstring stretch.
Description: From a front-leaning position, keeping the knees stiff, bring the feet up to the hands by inching forward with the toes. Then walk forward with the hands, keeping the feet and legs stiff and firmly planted.
Things to watch for: The children will want to walk with the hands and feet simultaneously. Emphasize that the hands should not move until the feet are perpendicular to the floor.

V-Sit

Level: Four years and older.
Purpose: Balance and abdominal strengthening.
Description: The youngster sits on the floor, placing the hands behind the rear end and lifting legs straight into the air. He then slowly lifts the hands off the floor to form a *V* and holds.
Things to watch for: It is very difficult to hold the *V* which takes concentration. In the beginning many children will roll back until the abdominal muscles are developed.

Bridge (Back Bend)

spotter

or initially

Level: Four years and older.

Purpose: Back and arm strength and coordination.

Description: The child lies on the floor on his back with knees bent. He places his hands (fingers pointing toward feet) above his shoulders and lifts the stomach, head, and hips upward, to form an arch.

Things to watch for: When first attempting the *Bridge*, most children will be able to lift the hips up but cannot raise the head and shoulders off the floor due to weak arm and abdominal muscles. Perform on a mat. Spotter may lift back up.

Squat Thrust

Level: Four years and older.

Purpose: Arm and leg strength.

Description: The youngster assumes a squatting position with the hands on the floor two feet in front of the feet. Placing his weight on his palms, he lifts the hips and jumps, pushing feet backward until the legs are extended. He then jumps forward, resuming the squatting position and stands. Repeat.

Things to watch for: Hands must stay firmly planted on the floor. The feet should be kicked backward and forward rather than dragged.

Rooster Hop

Level: Four years and older.

Purpose: Coordination and balance.

Description: Stand erect and hold the left leg with the right hand behind the right knee. Hop forward, backward, sideways. Repeat, using the other foot and hand. "Cock-a-doodle-doo" while hopping.

Things to watch for: Make sure all the children can hop before attempting the stunt. Have them extend the opposite hand to maintain balance and protect themselves if they fall forward.

Coffee Grinder

Level: Four years and older.
Purpose: Balance and arm strength.
Description: Start in a sitting position, legs extended, hands on the floor behind the hips. Roll to one side, supporting the weight on one hand and foot with the body in a straight line. Pivot around the supporting arm, taking small steps with the feet. Repeat on the other side.
Things to watch for: The arm may buckle up and the weight drop to the elbow. Keep the supporting arm and legs straight.

Partner Stunts

Seesaw

Level: Two-and-a-half years and older.
Purpose: Leg and stomach strength.
Description: Partners sit on the floor facing each other and grasping wrists. Their feet should be touching with the knees bent. As one partner leans forward, the other leans back.
Variation: Legs may be in a straddle position.
Things to watch for: Have children gently rock back and forth without jerking each other.

Wheelbarrow

Level: Four-and-a-half years and older.
Purpose: Strength and coordination.

Figure 82. A wheelbarrow.

Description: One child bends at his waist and places his palms on the floor. The partner steps between his feet and grasps his knees or ankles, lifting them off the floor. They both walk forward. Switch positions.

Things to watch for: Make sure the partner on the floor doesn't walk on his elbows. It is mandatory that the child holding the legs of his partner is larger and stronger.

Chinese Get-Up

Level: Four years and older.

Purpose: Coordination and leg strength.

Description: Children sit back to back with elbows hooked, knees bent, and feet flat on the floor. At the count of three, they push their feet into the floor and push their backs together, rising until they are in a standing position.

Variation: Once they're good at it (usually at age four-and-a-half or older), have the children raise half-way up and walk (one goes forward while the other goes backward).

Things to watch for: Children should be of equal weight so one doesn't lift the other onto his back. Have them raise straight up rather than leaning forward.

Wring The Towel

Level: Four years and older.
Purpose: Coordination.
Description: Children should be paired off by approximate size and weight. They join both hands and turn completely around by swinging the arms up and over their heads. Hands should always remain joined.
Things to watch for: Make sure the children turn toward the same side simultaneously. Partners should be of approximately the same height.

Leap Frog

Level: Four years and older.
Purpose: Development of large muscles.
Description: This may be done with partners or in a line formation using many "stones." The children line up, spaced four feet apart in a low squat with their arms wrapped around their knees and head down. They are the "stones." The "frog" starts at the end of the line. He puts his hands on the stones' backs and leaps with legs wide apart over them. The frog leaps over all the stones. At the end of the line, he becomes a stone and the first stone becomes a frog.
Things to watch for: The stones should remember to stay small and not lift their heads. The frog should leap high into the air by giving a push from his hands onto the stone.

Individual Tumbling Stunts

All tumbling, whether individual or partner, should be performed on mats. Each child is an individual and his ability will not always be equal to that of another person of his age. The instructor must remember this when teaching tumbling and may have to modify the program.

Forward Roll

Figure 83. For the Forward Roll the chin is tucked in . . .

*Figure 84.
. . . the feet push up . . .*

Figure 85. . . . and the child rolls onto the upper back.

Level: Three years and older.

Purpose: Balance and coordination.

Description: Squat down with toes on the edge of a mat and hands just outside the knees with fingers pointing forward. Tuck the chin to the chest, push off with the feet (lift hips up) onto the hands, and roll onto the upper back. End up on the feet in a squatting position.

Spotting techniques: Place one hand on the back of the child's neck and the other under his thighs. Lift the thighs up and keep the neck bent.

Things to watch for: The children may use the head to roll on; the head should never be used and should be kept close to the chest. When rolling over they may arch their backs instead of curling up.

Shoulder Roll

Level: Three-and-a-half years and older.

Purpose: Coordination and balance.

Description: From a crouched position, lean forward onto the hands and allow the arms to bend until the left shoulder lands on the mat. Raise the hips and roll onto the left shoulder, across the back and right hip, and onto the feet.

Spotting techniques: Kneel at the youngster's right side; place the left hand under his thighs and the right hand on his right shoulder. Simultaneously lift his hips and gently guide his shoulder to the left side.

Things to watch for: The child may end up in a *Log Roll* rather than lifting the hips as in a *Forward Roll*.

Backward Roll

Level: Four-and-a-half years and older.

Purpose: Coordination.

Description: From a squat stand, lean slightly forward and then rock backward onto the buttocks, across the back to a stand. The knees do not touch the mat and the legs are brought over the head. The hands are placed on either side of the head for a push.

Spotting techniques: The children may need to rock a number of times before they have built up enough momentum to roll over. The instructor should place one hand under the thighs (lift) and one under the neck. If a child is small, the spotter may stand over the child and lift the hips.

Things to watch for: Most children will roll to one side on a shoulder rather than push with both hands to lift the hips. Spotting is essential.

Tripod (Tip-Up)

Level: Four-and-a-half years and older.

Purpose: Balance.

Description: From a squatting position place the hairline of the head on the mat, with the hands under the shoulders and elbows bent, to form a triangle. Raise the hips as high as possible by walking the feet toward the hands. Place one knee on top of one elbow, and then the other knee on the other elbow. Hold.

Spotting techniques: Kneel next to the child placing one hand on his back and the other on the upper thigh (underside).

Things to watch for: The weight should be on the front (hairline) of the head, not the top; otherwise, the child will go into a forward roll. Make sure children walk up to their hands and don't thrust the legs to the elbows or a forward roll will occur.

Modified Cartwheel

Level: Four-and-a-half years and older.

Purpose: Coordination; developing arm strength.

Description: Have the children perform a *Donkey Kick*. Once the arms are strong enough to hold the body weight, attempt the *Modified Cartwheel*: They may place both hands simultaneously on the floor and push their legs to one side (modified). As they gain confidence, they will build up to a cartwheel (but not until at least five years of age).

Spotting techniques: Stand in front of the performer and grasp the hips as his hands contact the mat.

Things to watch for: Many children will be afraid of falling to one side and will bend their knees to compensate.

Variation: With the right side (or left) toward the mat, whip the right hand sideward and downward to the mat and follow it with the left hand. When explaining the stunt to the children, the instructor shouldn't use the terms *right* or *left*. Instead, she can say "one hand" or "other hand." The legs are swung upward, one at a time, over the head to the other side.

Head Stand

Level: Five years and older.

Purpose: Balance and concentration.

Description: The head stand is developed from the *Tripod* by lifting one leg up at a time into the air.

Spotting techniques: Stand behind the performer. As each leg is brought up, hold the ankles and place your ·knee into the child's back for support. A youngster may do the stunt himself by placing a mat next to a wall and using it to support his legs. Once balance is established, have him do the head stand alone.

Things to watch for: If the legs are brought up too fast, he will go into a forward roll. Make sure the hands are forming a triangle with the head for balance. Have the performer do a forward roll when coming out of the *Head Stand*.

Variations Of The Backward Roll

Level: Five years and older.

Figure 86. The Head Stand.

Purpose: Coordination.
Description:
1. Combination of forward and backward rolls; forward roll, pivot on feet, backward roll.
2. Series of backward rolls.
3. Straight stand to back roll; sit down with straight legs by dropping the weight to the hands.

Variations Of The Forward Roll

Level: Five years and older.
Purpose: Balance and coordination.
Description:
1. From stride stand position:

2. Squat and grasp ankles:

3. Raise right foot backward:

4. Forward rolls in succession.
5. Forward roll beginning and ending with stride stand.
6. Dive roll: short run, jump from both feet into a forward roll (be careful of neck).

Fish Flop

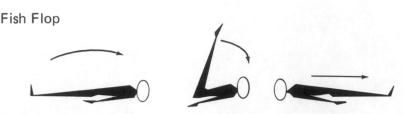

Level: Five years and older.
Purpose: Developing the back and abdominal muscles.
Description: Lie on back with hands at the sides. Kick the feet upward hard enough to bring the body onto the right shoulder (head should be turned to the left) and over to a lying position, face downward. As the legs are going over the head, arch the back, rolling onto the side of the face, chest, and abdomen.
Things to watch for: There will be a tendency to bring the legs up, rather than over the head. The children may land on their knees instead of their flat stomach and thighs. Remind them of a fish flopping when it's out of the water.

Partner Tumbling Stunts

When attempting partner stunts it is important to note that children should be of appropriate size for the intended skill. The child who is the base must be strong and large enough to properly support the top person. If the children are of approximately the same size, a double tumbling stunt will not be possible and will serve to frustrate both partners. If there is a shortage of larger students, the instructor should actively participate and become the base, or she may wish to eliminate some of the stunts due to their inappropriateness for her particular class.

Figure 87. The Angel Stand . . .

Figure 88. . . . is good for developing balance.

Angel Stand

Level: Two-and-a-half years and older. (If an adult is the base, any age child can perform the stunt. If another child is the base, do not attempt the *Angel Stand* until they are at least five years old.)

Purpose: Balance and teamwork; leg strengthening for the base.

Description: The base partner (*1*) lies on the floor on his back, facing his partner (*2*). *2* places *1*'s feet just above the hip bones (pointing outward). The partners join hands. At the count of three, *2* jumps forward and upward taking his feet off the ground, while *1* bends his knees and lifts *2* onto his feet. He straightens his legs. The arms joined help maintain balance. Once *2* is balanced, have him put his legs apart and let go with his hands (like an angel). The base (*1*) must be heavier than the top (*2*).

Spotting techniques: Stand to one side of the couple. Hold the shoulder and thigh on the top person to help the base get accustomed to the additional weight.

Things to watch for: When the top partner (*2*) takes his feet off the ground, make sure he doesn't go right over *1*'s head. The spotter should try to hold *2* until *1* has his legs straight.

Box Stand

Level: Two-and-a-half years if an adult is the base; five years if both partners are children.

Purpose: Arm strength (base) and balance.

Description: *2* (top) stands with feet apart over *1*'s head (lying down on back with legs straight up in air). *2* bends at the waist and grasps *1*'s ankles; *1* grasps *2*'s ankles. At the count of three, *2* raises his hips and legs off the floor while *1* lifts *2*'s ankles until his arms are straight, forming a box.

Spotting techniques: Stand to one side of the team and place the hands on *2*'s hips. At the count of three, help *2* lift his hips upward.

Things to watch for: The top child may lean too far forward instead of lifting upward and topple over the base. The base must lock his elbows and keep his arms straight.

Horizontal Stand

Level: Three years and older if an adult is the base. Don't attempt until at least five years of age if both partners are children.

Purpose: Arm and shoulder strength.

Description: One youngster (*1*) lies on his back with his knees bent and his feet flat on the floor. The top child (*2*) faces *1*'s knees, legs straddling the head. *1* grasps the shins of *2* while *2* leans forward and places his hands on *1*'s knees, with the arms straight. *1* lifts *2*'s legs until his arms are straight. *2* should keep the head up and body straight.

Spotting techniques: Stand to one side of the team, placing one hand around the top child's elbow and the other under his

Figure 89. The Horizontal Stand . . .

Figure 90. . . . develops arm and shoulder strength.

hips. Guide the hips upward and straighten the arm by pushing the elbow joint in with the thumb.

Things to watch for: If the elbows are not locked in place, both partners will lose their balance. Legs should be kept stiff and together.

Double Forward Roll

Level: May be done any time after a child can perform a good *Forward Roll* and arm strength is developed.

Purpose: Abdominal strength and coordination.

Description: One child (*1*) lies on a mat on his back; the other (*2*) stands straddling *1*'s head and facing his feet. They grasp each other's ankles. The roll begins with *2* doing a *Forward Roll*, carrying *1* up by the momentum. Continue the roll in that direction. Stress tucking the head down and landing on the shoulders and upper back.

Spotting techniques: Bend to one side of the team. Place one hand behind *2*'s head and the other behind his thighs.

Things to watch for: Make sure the partners hold onto each other's ankles at all times. When the top person leans forward, have him tuck his head immediately and bend at the waist to prevent him from flying forward between the base's legs.

Pyramids

Level: Six years and older (two levels only for five-year-olds).

Purpose: Teamwork and balance.

Description: There are any number of variations that can be best shown through stick-figure illustration. The easiest one to perform is to have the strongest children kneel side by side. The second row climbs up and kneels on the backs of the first row and so on. After the pyramid is built, have the children

Figure 91. After the Pyramid is built . . .

Figure 92. . . . the children "squash" down.

"squash" down on the count of three by extending the arms forward and the legs backward.

Spotting techniques: Help the children up onto the backs of the other youngsters. Hold the elbow of the top person when the "squash" takes place.

Things to watch for: Have the upper children put one knee on the upper back of one child and their other knee on the next child below him. Make sure they all "squash" at the same time.

Have children wearing glasses remove them before attempting the Pyramid.

Variations:

Chapter 9

Relay Races (For Youngsters Four-And-A-Half To Five Years)

The activities discussed thus far in this text have dealt with many areas that include individual development, body awareness, following directions, and group play. Children move at their own tempo and in their own way. When dealing with relays, the emphasis is placed upon fun, socialization, decision making, the opportunity to exercise basic skills, and competition. Relays involve repetition and the development of the basic locomotor patterns (see chapter 4); relating to a partner or objects; or going over, under, or around small equipment.

Circle games are appropriate for initial experiences; the children seem to relate to the structural security in this kind of formation. Relays are generally conducted in a line formation and shouldn't be introduced until the youngster feels more secure with his peers and with his own abilities (usually not until the age of four-and-a-half to five years).

Most texts on physical education do not include relays for the younger child. Granted, the two- and three-year-old is not ready either physiologically or emotionally for them but it is this writer's opinion that if a four to five-year-old youngster has had a good development of motor skills in early childhood physical education and has a positive self-image, he will be able to perform simple races with little difficulty.

COMPETITION

It is important at this point to discuss the varying schools of thought dealing with self-image, competition, and relationship with peers—essentially, what relays are all about.

One school believes that as the child becomes more autonomous, he should be exposed to the positive side of life, thus building up his self-image. The development of a child's self-esteem is the most important thing. It sets the foundation for a fairly well-adjusted adult. Anderson and Anderson believe that "Sympathetic behavior increases during the preschool years and also shows wide individual differences."[1] Smart and Smart state, "Preschool children's consideration for others develops most readily when parents do the asserting of power over their children while pointing out the consequences of children's behavior toward other people . . . Children should be encouraged to learn a sense of sharing an intimacy with each other. Growth in social behavior comes not from imposing one's will on others or submitting to a stronger person but from perceiving the other person's needs and desires and letting him understand yours."[2] They also believe that "The sense of autonomy is promoted by clear, firm guidance which permits successful decision making within the limits it imposes. The opposite of a sense of autonomy includes feelings of shame and doubt."[3]

Erik H. Erikson believes that ". . . These negative feelings creep in when the youngster cannot choose and act independently enough, when the results of his choices and actions are disastrous, and when adults use shaming as a method of control. Many adults use this technique as a discipline device."[4]

When a child is ashamed, he is embarrassed and does not want to be seen. This technique does not encourage good behavior but rather defiance and a feeling of worthlessness on the part of the child. Many authorities feel that competition supports negative feelings of shame and guilt and does not support a sense of autonomy.

On the other hand, a second school of thought supports competition as the natural outcome of jealousy. It is my opinion that teamwork and competition, if channeled in a positive direction in the form of relays and games, can aid in autonomy. This will be fully explained later. Let us first discuss the supportive evidence of the second school.

Dr. Haim Ginott states that "Jealousy originates in an infant's desire to be his mother's only 'dearly beloved'. This desire is so possessive that it tolerates no rivals. When brothers and sisters arrive, the child competes with them for the exclusive love of both parents. The competition may be open or hidden, depending on the parent's attitudes toward jealousy."[5]

Readers may question by asking, what if there are no siblings? But there will be competition for the mother's love with anyone who poses a threat (father, grandparent, aunt). Since a child cannot be the sole receiver of this love, it is inevitable that jealousy will occur.

Ginott goes on to say that "The bitter fruits of unresolved childhood rivalries are all around us in adult life. They can be seen in the irrational rivalry of the man who cannot gracefully lose a ping-pong game, or who is always ready to bet his life and fortune in order to prove a point. They can also be seen in the man who shuns all competition, who feels defeated before a struggle begins, who does not stand up even for his legitimate rights. Thus sibling rivalry affects a child's life more than is realized. It may indelibly stamp his personality and distort his character."[6] He adds, "Normally, children feel jealous of brothers and sisters. They may feel that their siblings receive more love and may vie with them for affection. But when love is given, they are readily assured. They too, may like competition and excelling, but they can also enjoy games for the fun of playing. Moreover, they can accept defeat without much pain or strain. . . .

Children do not question the existence of jealousy in the family. Jealousy, envy, and rivalry will inevitably be there. To fail to anticipate them, or to be shocked at their appearance, is an ignorance that is far from bliss."[7,8]

Smart and Smart, in their book *Children: Development and Relationships*, state that "Parents' approval and resulting rewards often depend on how the child compares with his siblings, as well as with children outside the family. To look good and thereby be most approved and loved, he has to be better than someone else, other than his brother or sister."[9] Is this not the essence of competition?

Competition becomes more evident in the preschool period. Leuba used a peg board situation with which preschool children played either singly or in pairs. The number of pegs placed properly in these two settings was compared. Two-year-olds

were little affected by the presence of other children. Three-
and four-year-olds, while competitive, were so distracted that
they did more poorly when working in pairs than singly.
Five-year-olds were not only competitive, but also increased
their output. In the second study the investigator encouraged a
child to use building blocks competitively in creating something
bigger and (later) prettier than that of his companion. Using
several standards of rivalry, she found no competitive reponses
for children aged two and three, 43 percent for children three
and four, 69 percent for children aged four and five, 75 percent
for ages five to six, and 86 percent for the six- and seven-year-
olds.[10,11]

Young children are not particularly competitive, but, in our
culture at least, children become progressively more competitive
as age increases. This reflects the assimilation of the competitive
value of our society. The limitations of the study should be
discussed. Making something "bigger and prettier" may not
have been comprehended by the two-year-old and as a result, he
did not compete. If the task was understood, he too might have
competed. Nonetheless, competition does increase with age as
comprehension becomes greater.

It should also be noted that the word *competition* doesn't
always deal in terms of others. It deals with self. If a child
attempts to do better today than he did yesterday, he is using
himself as the competitor. The child of five and older is physiologically and psychologically capable of doing this (see chapter 1). It is directing what may be considered by some as a negative force into a positive one by using a different focal point.

It is this writer's opinion that both schools of thought can be
joined to create a happy situation. It is not an *if . . . then*
proposition. Let us study the facts:
  1. Jealousy is natural;
  2. Competition is inevitable;
  3. The American culture is geared around competition;
  4. Most children develop a sense of autonomy;
  5. Autonomy encourages decision making.
Games and relays, if taught by a competent and sympathetic
instructor, encourage competition and autonomy. They will
channel the negative into the positive by making winning and
losing *secondary* until the child has developed self-confidence
(Stress upon winning and losing can be handled in later grades.)

The primary emphasis should be on fun and socialization, and on putting the basic skills into a game situation and decision making.

It is my opinion that psychologists make such an issue of losing that suddenly people feel that it's *terrible* to lose. They are failures; they are shamed. But they should not feel that way! Competition is a natural part of life and should be integrated into every preschool program to give the youngster a positive foundation built upon the handling of defeats as well as successes. If he is not exposed to defeats until the age of seven or eight, as some authorities suggest, he may not be able to cope and will become totally devastated by the experience.

SPORTSMANSHIP

It is essential that early in his experiences a child learn the importance of sportsmanship. Clean competition is imperative in any game situation. This is where sportsmanship enters into the picture.

A good self-image is extremely important. If a child has tried with all his might and loses to someone with better ability, he should not feel permanently defeated. He must try again and again, slowly improving and gaining importance and self worth. *Note*: this need not be overly emphasized for the younger child.

For this reason, the teacher or parent conducting a race must remember to place children of approximately the same size and ability against one another. A child who loses to a far superior individual (athletically) will feel ashamed, hurt, and mad; yet a youngster who wins with no good competition has gained little for his self-esteem. The challenge should be there.

A child should be taught not to ridicule a slower youngster or a losing teammate. Compassion should be stressed. There has to be a winner and a loser in every competitive event. Children will have their turn at each but must remember there will always be a "next time."

TEAMWORK

Competition, loyalty, compassion, and sportsmanship all make up teamwork. True, the children are entering races as individuals, but they are also part of a team. They must stick together and praise each other for an all-out effort. It is their responsibility (and this should be taught at a young age) to encourage each other.

OBJECTIVES OF RELAY RACES

1. To develop skill in basic movements.
2. To have fun for fun's sake.
3. To learn positive forms of competition.
4. To learn the early forms of basic teamwork.
5. To aid in the development of decision making and problem solving.
6. To aid in the socialization process.

As previously stated, most four-and-a-half- to five-year-olds are ready, both physically and emotionally, to handle relays. Each race should be carefully selected for the ability level of the youngsters in that class. All the listed relays may be modified or expanded as the teacher desires.

PRACTICAL SUGGESTIONS
FOR CONDUCTING RELAYS

1. Place four to eight youngsters on a team. Too many on a team drags out the race and they will lose interest. In some races it will also add too much confusion (e.g., when passing ball over and under).
2. If the teams have uneven numbers, have the first (and strongest) child also be the last. The other alternative is to have the extras wait out a turn and become judges with the teacher.
3. Define starting lines, turning points, and finishing acts. In some cases a race is ended when the last person completes his turn. In others, it is not ended until an entire team is seated. A definite finishing act eliminates argument as to the winner.
4. The instructor should be a line judge. It is not fair to ask a youngster to determine his friend's fate if a line is not reached.
5. Have the *instructor* set up the teams. Make sure that the teams are equally divided and that the youngsters are competing against children with equal abilities (i.e., John on Team *A* is running against Bill on Team *B*, and both these boys have similar expertise).

6. Selections of relays should initially be simple. As a guideline, choose or create relays that contain no more than two steps (for children ages four through seven).

7. Line up children in the selected teams. Describe relay. Walk once or twice through the relay course and ask if there are any questions. If a child looks puzzled, ask him if he has any specific questions.

Skills

There are some basic concepts in relays that each child should be made familiar with before attempting the races. They are fairly simple concepts but should be discussed in full in case children have questions.

1. Ready to run position: One foot is forward with knees bent and body weight slightly forward.

2. Running, hopping, jumping: (see chapter 4, "Basic Movements").

3. Tagging: Emphasize touch-tag, not pushing or shoving. This can be accomplished by suggesting that the children keep the left hand out to the side with an open palm.

4. Turning and running: Emphasize pivot on the ball of the foot (see also chapter 5, "Variations").

5. Overrunning the finish line: Be sure to discuss the importance of running, slipping, sliding, etc., full-speed past the finish line. Some children may have the tendency to slow down since they literally interpret the command "Stop at the finish line" to mean just that. Have the rest of the team move to one side (the same side) to make room for the runner.

Safety Tips

1. Relay lines should be well spaced between teams.

2. Make sure running areas are clear of all obstacles to prevent injuries.

3. Have starting, turning, and finishing lines well marked.

4. Use safe objects (i.e., balls or pieces of cloth) in passing relays. Don't use sticks. A child may fall onto the object or into another player and an accident could occur.

5. Children wearing glasses should have them taped around the head, wear safety shields, or remove them (if they can perform as well without them).

TYPES OF RELAYS

Semi-Stationary Relay

Children stand, sit, or kneel in a line and pass an object over their heads, under the legs, etc., to the person behind them. When the last person in line receives the object, he runs to the front of the line, becomes first, and continues the same skill.

Line Relay

Children line up one behind the other. They run to or around a given spot and come back to their team, tagging the hand of the next person in line. After completing a turn, each child becomes the last until he is eventually back in his original position.

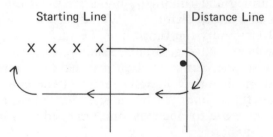

Obstacle Relay

Each team forms a single file. Obstacles (such as cones or tires) are placed on the floor a short distance from the starting line and equal-distance apart. On a given signal, the first player moves to the right of the first object, to the left of the second, and around the last and then weaves in the same manner back to the starting line, tagging the next player.

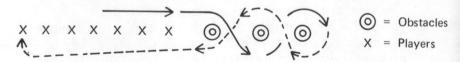

Circle Relays

Two or more circles composed of the same number of players compete in running, skipping, hopping, or walking events, each child tagging the person next to him after he has run around his circle.

Variations

Stunt Relays

Children may act out different animals, carry objects between their knees, or hum a song while running.

Locomotor

Children run, hop, skip, jump, tiptoe, or gallop individually in a line formation.

General Hints

1. Make sure that all contestants cross the starting line before the next players continue the race.
2. If in any of the relay races a tie occurs, have the team sitting in the straightest line become the winner.
3. Unless otherwise stated, the children completing their turns go to the end of the line. The winning team is that which is first to complete the skills and be back in the original position.

Note: It is important to mention that all of the following relays can be expanded for children *older* than four-and-a-half to five years of age. Each class will differ in ability, and no hard, fast rules should be made. Some children will not be able to handle particular skills while others will find them a simple task. This writer recommends that each teacher use his or her own discretion regarding the handling of relay races.

If relays will enhance the class's activities and the skills of the children, then by all means incorporate them into the physical education program. If they will not, eliminate them.

Semi-Stationary Relays

Over-Under Relay

Level: Five years and older.

Figure 93. Children performing the Over- . . .

Figure 94. . . . Under relay.

Purpose: Following directions and the development of eye-hand coordination.

Equipment: Playground balls.

Organization: Divide the class into equal teams and have team members stand one behind the other in file formation. The first player passes the ball over his head to the player directly in back of him. Player two receives the ball and passes it under his legs to player three. This continues until the last player receives the ball. He then runs around the right side of the team, becoming the first player and passing the ball over his head to the second child. This continues until all players have had a turn at being first. The team which lines up in the original order first is the winner.

Things to watch for: Each child receiving the ball will have to switch the method of passing it to the rear. He may also have difficulty in remembering to run to the front of the line and may hand the ball to the second player rather than passing it over his head.

Under-Relay

Level: Four-and-a-half years and older.

Purpose: Development of eye-hand coordination and following directions.

Equipment: Playground balls.

Organization: Divide the class into equal teams and have them line up in single file. The first player passes the ball between his legs to the second. The ball is passed, not rolled, under all the legs of the children. The last person receiving the ball runs around to the right side, becoming first and continuing the same skill. The first team to line up in the original order is the winner.

Things to watch for: Make sure the children pass the ball from hand to hand. There will be a tendency for the team to roll it on the floor as the excitement builds.

Bridge Relay

Level: Four-and-a-half years and older.

Purpose: Coordination and change of level.

Equipment: None.

Organization: Divide the class into equal teams and have them line up in single file. The children spread their feet in a straddle position. At a signal, the last child in each line drops to his knees and crawls between the legs of his teammates until he reaches the front of the line. Then he stands up and assumes the straddle position. As soon as a child becomes the last in line, he starts crawling. The first team to line up in the original order is the winner.

Things to watch for: Smaller children may be lifted off the floor by the crawler if he is larger.

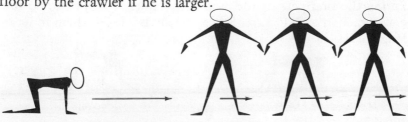

Running And Variation Relays

Run, Rabbit, Run

Level: Four-and-a-half years and older.

Purpose: Change of direction and the development of basic rhythms.

Equipment: None.

Organization: Divide the class into equal teams and have them line up in single file formation. Mark a starting and a distance line thirty feet apart. The teams line up behind the starting line. At a given signal, the first players run to the distance line, pivot, and hop back, tagging the second players. The first player takes his place at the end of the line. The team which completes the race first and is then seated is the winner.

Things to watch for: Some of the children will end up jumping rather than hopping. Children must remain behind the starting line until tagged.

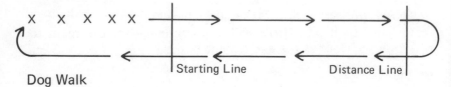

Starting Line   Distance Line

Dog Walk

Level: Four-and-a-half years and older.

Purpose: Development of variations of the basic movements.

Equipment: None.

Organization: Mark a starting and a distance line thirty feet apart. Divide the class into equal teams and have them form a single file. The first players crawl to the distance line, pivot, and return in a *Dog Walk* back to the second players. (A *Dog Walk* is performed by keeping the body weight on the palms and feet with the legs straight facing the floor.) The team which completes the race first and has all its members seated behind the starting line is the winner.

Things to watch for: Emphasize that the children crawl during the first part of the race. The tendency will be to do the entire race in a *Dog Walk*. It may be advisable for them to wear long pants.

Crawl   Dog Walk

Figure 95. The Crab Walk relay.

Crab Walk Relay

Level: Four-and-a-half years and older.
Purpose: Develop coordination; increase arm and leg strength.
Equipment: None.
Organization: Mark a starting and a distance line thirty feet apart. Divide the class into equal teams and have them single file. The first players gallop (see chapter 4) to the distance line, then sit on the floor, doing a *Crab Walk* back to the second players. The *Crab Walk* is accomplished by facing away from the direction one is heading, body weight on the palms and feet, knees bents, and the tummy facing upward. The first team to complete the race and be seated behind the starting line is the winner.

Things to watch for: The children may drag their rear ends on the floor rather than lifting the hips. If correctly performed, the exercise is excellent for developing the thigh and abdominal muscles. Make sure the players look behind them when doing the crab walk to prevent walking into a wall or another person.

Lift right foot and left hand and step *backward*. Repeat using left foot and right hand.

Tiptoe Tinker Bell

Level: Four-and-a-half years and older.
Purpose: Development of the arch and toe muscles.
Equipment: None.
Organization: Draw a starting and a distance line thirty feet apart. Divide the class into equal teams and have them in single file. At a given signal, the first players tiptoe to the distance line and tiptoe backward until they reach the second players. The first team to have all its members complete the race and be seated behind the starting line is the winner.

Things to watch for: Since it does take strong foot muscles to tiptoe for a distance, the children may tire easily and walk with the entire foot. Tell them to keep the hands extended to the sides for balance.

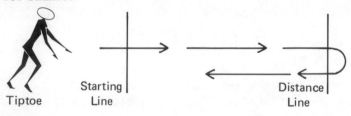

Tiptoe   Starting   Distance
              Line   Line

Ball Relays

All the ball relays should have:
1. Marked starting and distance lines approximately thirty feet apart;
2. The class equally divided into teams and standing in file formation;
3. A given signal for starting the race.

Bounce Relay

Level: Four-and-a-half years and older.
Purpose: Eye-hand coordination.
Equipment: Playground balls.
Organization: At a given signal the first players run with the ball to the distance line, stop, bounce the ball three times, and run back to the second players. The first team to finish is declared the winner.

Note: This is an excellent introduction to relay races. It is simple, yet teaches children the basics of competition, teamwork, and direction-following.

Balloon Push

Level: Four to four-and-a-half years and older.

Purpose: Eye-hand coordination.

Equipment: Beach balls or balloons.

Organization: At a signal, the first players must tap the balloons or balls to the distance line, tap them back, and hand them to the next child in line. The balloon should not touch the floor. If it does, the player must go back to the starting line and begin again. This continues until one team has finished and is declared the winner.

Note: Four-year-olds and older can be expected to perform this skill fairly well.

Back Ball

Level: Four-and-a-half years and older.

Purpose: Coordination and direction-following.

Equipment: Playground balls four inches in diameter, if available.

Organization: The first child in each line runs to the distance line holding the ball behind his back. At the distance line, he puts the ball between his knees and returns to the starting line before giving the ball to the next player. The team which finishes first and is seated wins.

Variation: The relay may be simplified by having the players run back holding the ball in their hands instead of between the knees.

Things to watch for: Make sure the ball is not too big for the youngsters.

Over-Under Relay

(see *Semi-Stationary Relays*).

Under-Relay

(see *Semi-Stationary Relays*).

Dribble Relay

Level: Five years and older.

Purpose: Eye-hand coordination.

Equipment: Playground balls six to eight inches in diameter.

Organization: At a given signal the first players bounce the ball to the distance line and back to the second players. The first team to complete the skill and to be seated behind the starting line is the winner.

Things to watch for: The teacher should allow the children to bounce the ball with one or both hands. Make sure they bounce the ball with every step taken. Some children will hold the ball and run instead of dribbling it.

Soccer Relay

Level: Five years and older.
Purpose: Foot coordination and foot-muscle development.
Equipment: Playground balls.
Organization: At the starting signal, the first players push the ball on the floor with the insides of their feet to the distance line and back to the second players. The first team finished and seated wins.
Things to watch for: When first attempting the soccer relay, the children may kick the ball with their toes. Work on the soccer dribble before attempting the relay.

Wall Ball

Level: Five years and older.
Purpose: Eye-hand coordination.
Equipment: Playground balls and a wall.
Organization: At a given signal, the first players run with the ball to a predetermined wall, throw the ball against the wall, and catch it. Having completed the skill, they run back to the second players. The first team to finish wins.
Variation: Older children can do any number of combinations, such as clapping one time or pivoting before catching the ball. These can be made as simple or complex as the class level.
Things to watch for: Allow the children to let the ball bounce after it hits the wall. The underhand pass should be taught before attempting this race (see chapter 6, *Ball Activities*).

Kangaroo Race

Level: Five years and older.
Purpose: Coordination and balance.
Equipment: Playground balls four inches in diameter, if available.
Organization: At a given signal, the first players put the ball between their knees (or thighs) and either walk or jump to the

Figure 96. Kangaroo race.

distance line and back to the second players. The team completing the race first is the winner.

Things to watch for: If the balls are too large they may pop out of place. Some children may need to hold the balls while jumping. Older children (five-and-a-half years and older) should be told that if the ball drops to the floor they must repeat the race at the starting line.

Obstacle Relays

All obstacle relays should have:
1. Marked starting and distance lines approximately thirty to forty feet apart;
2. A given starting signal;
3. Equally divided teams standing in single file;
4. A winner declared when one team finishes the required skills and is seated behind the starting line.

Tire Relay

Level: Four-and-a-half years and older.
Purpose: Coordination and direction-following.
Equipment: Automobile tires (three per team).
Organization: Three tires are placed equal distances apart in front of each team. At a given signal, the first players run to the

right of the first tire, to the left of the second tire, and around the last. The weave back in the same manner to the second players waiting at the starting line. The team finishing first is declared the winner.

Variation

Things to watch for: The players may have trouble going around the tires. Walk all teams through a practice session once or twice before racing.

Cone Relay

Level: Four-and-a-half years and older.
Purpose: Coordination and direction-following.
Equipment: Rubber cones used in road repair work.
Organization: This is handled in the same manner as the *Tire Relay*. It can be simple or complex depending upon the skills performed.
Variations: Children may jump over the cones; go entirely around the cones; crawl or run backwards around the cones; or

Figure 97. Cone relay.

pick up cones and place them at the distance line while the next player picks up the pile and respaces the cones.

Runaway Tire Race

Level: Five years and older.
Purpose: Coordination and balance.
Equipment: Automobile tires.
Organization: The first person on each team holds (balances) a tire upright on the floor. At a given signal he must roll the tire around to a given point and back to the next team member. The first team to finish wins.
Things to watch for: The tire should not be too heavy for the youngster or, if it falls, he will not be able to lift it back to the upright position without help. If the tire drops, ask the players to right it and continue along to the distance or starting line.

Tire Jumping

Level: Four-and-a-half years and older.
Purpose: Coordination and agility.
Equipment: Automobile tires.
Organization: Two or more tires are placed twenty feet from the starting line and equal distance apart. At a given signal, the first players must run and jump over each tire, cross the distance line, and return, jumping over the tires, back to the

Figure 98. The Tire Jumping relay.

starting line and second players. The first team that is finished and seated wins.

Things to watch for: Encourage the children to jump with the feet together. They should practice jumping before the race.

Stunt Relays

Three-Legged Race

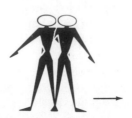

Level: Four-and-a-half years and older.
Purpose: Working with a partner and coordination.
Equipment: Strips of cloth two feet long.
Organization: The children are divided equally into teams and form pairs. A starting and a distance line are marked thirty feet apart. The first two partners (of approximately the same height) grasp each other around the waist or shoulders with the inside arm. Their inside legs are loosely tied by a two-foot strip of soft material. At the starting signal, the first pair in each line steps forward with the outside feet followed by the inside tied feet. The children walk in this manner to the distance line and back to the starting line, tagging the second pair who continue in the same manner. The first team to finish wins.

Things to watch for: The children should practice the walk before starting the race. It must be emphasized that the team must walk as a unit. It may be helpful if the children count out loud as the steps are taken.

Singing Relay

Level: Four to four-and-a-half years and older.
Purpose: Enjoyment and learning a song.
Equipment: None.
Organization: The children are equally divided into teams and stand single file behind the starting line. At a given signal, they must run to the distance line (where the instructor is standing) and sing a short song. On completing the verse, they run back and tag the second player. The team finishing first wins.

Note: Review a number of songs such as *Twinkle, Twinkle, Little Star; Batman;* or *I'm A Little Teapot* with the class before the race.

Name and Address Relay

Level: Four-and-a-half years and older.
Purpose: Memory testing.
Equipment: None.
Organization: Children line up by teams in a single file formation behind the starting line. On a given signal, the first players run to the instructor (approximately 25-30 feet from starting line) and say their names, addresses, and mother's and father's (or guardian's) first names. They run back to their team and tag the second players. The first team to complete the task and be seated is declared the winner.

Dressing Relay

Level: Four to four-and-a-half years and older.
Purpose: Coordination.
Equipment: Old, large clothing (donated) requiring no zippers or buttons—for example, housedresses, large overalls, or bathrobes.
Organization: A large box of old clothing is placed in front of each team at the distance line. Beginning from behind the starting line, the first players must run to the box, put on an outfit (hats, dress, pants, etc.), and run back to the starting line. They disrobe and hand their outfits to the second players. The second players must put on the outfit, run to the distance line, take off the outfit, and run back to tag the third players. This continues until one team is finished and is declared the winner.
Note: Have clothing that is easy to put on and take off. An old pillow case with holes for the arms and head will do nicely. This is an extremely funny relay and terrific for rainy days or camp situations.

Log Roll Relay

Level: Four-and-a-half years and older.
Purpose: Change of level and coordination.
Equipment: Mats, which are placed opposite each team at the distance line.
Organization: Children line up, by teams, in single file formation behind the starting line. On a given signal, the first

players must run to the mats, do a *Log Roll*, and run back to tag the second players.

Variation: Any stunt or combination of stunts may be performed, depending upon the age and ability of the class (make sure there is a spotter present at each mat).

Things to watch for: Practice the chosen skill before starting the race. Make sure all the children can easily perform it. Partner stunts (i.e., *Chinese Get-Up, Wheelbarrow*) may also be included.

Round-The-Bases Relay

Level: Five years and older.
Purpose: Direction-following.
Equipment: Four bases.
Organization: Mark out a baseball diamond either on a playing field or in a game room. Divide the class into two teams, and have one team line up behind home plate with the other behind second base. At a given signal, the first person in each line runs around the four bases. As soon as he returns to the starting point, the second player starts running. Runners must touch the bases; if they fail to do so, they must go back and touch them before continuing. The first team lined up in the original order is the winner.

Things to watch for: Mark the bases in tape or, if outside, with flat pieces of heavy rubber. The children must know the direction to run. Standing in the center field allows the instructor to see all bases. If need be, she should use a volunteer parent as a base judge.

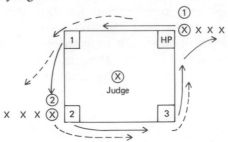

Notes to Chapter 9

1. H. H. Anderson and G. L. Anderson, "Social Development," ed. L. Carmichael, *Manual of Child Psychology* (New York: Wiley, 1954).

2. Mollie S. Smart and Russell C. Smart, *Children, Development, and Relationships*, rev. ed. (New York: Macmillan, 1972).
3. Ibid.
4. Erik H. Erikson, *Childhood and Society*, rev. ed. (New York: Norton, 1964).
5. Haim G. Ginott, *Between Parent and Child* (New York: Macmillan, 1965, and Avon Books, 1973).
6. Ibid.
7. Ibid.
8. Ibid.
9. Smart and Smart, *Children, Development, and Relationships,* rev. ed.
10. Pearl J. Greenberg, "Competition in Children: An Experimental Study," *American Journal of Psychology* 44(1932).
11. C. Leuba, "An Experimental Study of Rivalry in Children," *Journal of Comparative Psychology* 16(1933).

Glossary

Agility: the ability to change directions swiftly, easily, and under good control.

Apparatus: large playground items of a more or less fixed nature such as jungle gym, balance beam, trampoline.

Balance: the ability to maintain body equilibrium in a variety of positions.

Cognitive Development: the creation of interesting ideas, problems, questions.

Coordination: the harmonious functioning of muscles in producing complex movement.

Endurance: the ability to carry on muscular effort over a period of time.

Equipment: (small supplies): small, movable supplies such as balls, cones, tires, dumbbells.

Flexibility: the range of movement at the joints.

Hamstring: one of the muscles at the back of the knee.

Large Muscle Movement: activities primarily concerned with developing the large skeletal muscles found in the arms, legs, and trunk (i.e., running, jumping, hopping, skipping).

Movement Exploration: investigating the unknown through creative movement.

Parallel Play: engaging at the same time in the same activity as someone else but without interaction.

Perceptual-Motor Learning: act of receiving information from stimuli of the senses, processing the information, and responding to its meaning through movement.

Physical Development: development of growth and fitness of the body into harmonious movement.

Readiness: the physiological and psychological capacity to handle specific situations or skills.

Sense of Autonomy: development of the sense of self built upon the foundation of trust, love, and guidelines.

Sensorimotor Development: during the period from one to eighteen months, when the infant moves, mouths, touches, and looks to build concepts of his body and his surroundings.

Spatial Awareness: the development of physical self-awareness and the relationship to surroundings.

Speed: the ability to move quickly and effectively.

Spotter: an assistant to the performer who guides him through an activity.

Small Muscles Movement: activities primarily concerned with developing the small skeletal muscles (i.e., fingers, toes, head, neck).

Strength: the development of muscles through stress and tension applied during exercise.

Stride-Stand: standing with legs shoulder distance apart.

Vitality: energy.

Bibliography

Ames, Louise Bates, and Ilg, Frances. *Parents Ask*. New York: Harper & Row, 1962.

Ames, Louise Bates. *Child Behavior*. New York: Harper & Row, 1955, paperback, 1972.

_____. "The Development of the sense of Time in the Young Child." *Journal of Genetic Psychology* 68(1946): 97-125.

Anderson, J. E. "The Relation of Attitude to Adjustment." *Education* 73(1952): 210-218.

Anderson, Marian; Elliot, Margaret E.; and LaBerge, Jenne. *Play with a Purpose: Elementary School Physical Education*. New York: Harper & Row, 1972.

Anderson, Robert H., and Shone, Harold G. *Readings in Early Childhood Education. As the twig Is Bent*. Boston: Houghton Mifflin, 1972.

Andrews, Gladys; Saurborn, Jeanette; and Schneider, Elsa. *Physical Education for Today's Boys and Girls*. Boston: Allyn and Bacon, 1960.

Beard, Ruth. *An Outline of Piaget's Developmental Psychology for Students and Teachers*. New York: Basic Books, 1969, New America Library, 1972.

Bieri, Arthur Peter. *Action Games*. Belmont, California: Fearon Pubs., 1972.

Block, Susan D. "The Preschool Physical Education Program: Its Importance and Aims." *The Bulletin, Connecticut Journal of Health, Physical Education and Recreation* 22, 1(1975): 16-18.

Breckenridge, M. E., and Murphy, M.D. *Growth and Development of the Young Child*. 8th ed. Philadelphia: W. B. Saunders, 1969.

Broer, Marion. *Efficiency of Human Movement*. 3rd ed. Philadelphia: W. B. Saunders, 1973.

Bronfenbrenner, Urie. "Origins of Alienation." *Scientific American*. August 1974.

Bruner, J. S., and Goodman, C. C. "Value and Need as Organizing Factors in Perception." *Journal of Abnormal and Social Psychology* 42(1947): 33-44.

Bryant, Rosealie, and Eloise McLean Oliver. *Complete Elementary Physical Education Guide*. New York: Parker, 1974.

Caplan, Frank, and Theresa Caplane. *The Power of Play*. New York: Anchor Press/Doubleday, 1974.

Carr, Rachel. *Creative Yoga Exercises for Children: Be a Frog, a Bird, or a Tree*. New York: Doubleday, 1973.

Committee of California School Supervisors Association. *Guiding the Young Child*. Boston: D. C. Heath, 1959.

Committee on Understanding and Knowledge in Physical Education. *Knowledge and Understanding in Physical Education.* Washington, D.C.: American Association for Health, Physical Education and Recreation, 1973.

Cratty, Bryant J. *Intelligence in Action.* Englewood Cliffs, New Jersey: Prentice-Hall, 1973.

————. *Movement Behavior and Motor Learning.* 3rd ed. Philadelphia: Lea and Febiger, 1973.

————. *Teaching Motor Skills.* Englewood Cliffs, New Jersey: Prentice-Hall, 1973.

Cratty, Bryant J., and Martin, Sister Margaret Mary. *Perceptual-Motor Efficiency in Children: The Measurement and Improvement of Movement Attributes.* Philadelphia: Lea and Febiger, 1969.

Dauer, Victor, and Robert P. Pangrazi. *Dynamic Physical Education for Elementary School Children.* 5th ed. Minneapolis, Minnesota: Burgess, 1975.

Denenberg, Victor H. *Education of the Infant and Young Child.* New York: Academic Press, 1970.

Diem, Liselott. *Who Can.* Germany: Wilhelm Lipert Publisher, 1964.

_____. *Kinder Lernen Sport.* Germany: Kosel-Verlag Gmbtt. and Co., 1974.

_____. *Sport im Ibis 3 Lebensjahr.* Germany: Kosel-Verlag Gmbtt. and Co., 1974.

Drowatzky, John N. *Motor Learning: Principles and Practices.* Minneapolis, Minnesota: Burgess, 1975.

Drury, Blanche Jessen, and Schmid, Andrea Bodo. *Gymnastics for Women.* Palo Alto, California: Mayfield, 1970.

Eckert, Helen M., and Espenschade, Anna S. *Motor Development.* Columbus, Ohio: Charles E. Merrill, 1967.

Elkind, David. *A Sympathetic Understanding of the Child: Birth to 16.* Boston: Allyn & Bacon, 1974.

Erikson, Erik H. *Childhood and Society.* New York: Norton, 1964.

Ewing, Neil. *Games, Stunts, and Exercises.* Belmont, California: Fearon Pubs., 1964.

Fait, Hollis F. *Physical Education for the Elementary School Child.* Philadelphia: W. B. Saunders, 1971.

Flavell, J. H. *The Developmental Psychology of Jean Piaget.* Princeton, New Jersey: D. Van Nostrand, 1963.

Flinchum, Betty M. *Motor Development in Early Childhood.* Saint Louis: C. V. Mosby, 1975.

Gesell, Arnold, and Ilg, Frances. *Child Development: An Introduction to the Study of Human Growth.* New York: Harper and Brothers, 1940.

Gesell, Arnold. *Studies in Child Development.* New York and London: Harper and Brothers, 1948, Greenwood, 1972.

_____. *The First Five Years of Life.* New York: Harper and Brothers, 1940.

Getman, G. N. *How to Develop Your Child's Intelligence.* Penna: Research Publications, 1962.

Gilliom, Bonnie Cherp. *Basic Movement Education for Children: Rationale and Teaching Units.* Reading, Massachusetts: Addison-Wesley, 1970.

Ginott, Haim G. *Between Parent and Child.* New York: Macmillan, 1965, Avon Books, 1973.

Greenberg, Pearl J. "Competition in Children: An Experimental Study." *American Journal of Psychology* 44(1932): 221-248.

Gruenberg, Sidonie Matsner. *The New Encyclopedia of Child Care and Guidance.* Garden City, New York: Doubleday, 1968.

Hackett, Layne C., and Robert Jenson. *A Guide to Movement Exploration.* Palo Alto, California: Peek Publications, 1973.

Halsey, Elizabeth, and Porter, Lorena. *Physical Education for Children.* New York, Chicago: Holt, Rinehart & Winston, 1963.

Hess, Robert D., and Doreen Craft. *Teachers of Young Children.* Boston: Houghton Mifflin, 1975.

Hendrick, Joanne. *The Whole Child: New Trends in Early Education.* Saint Louis: C. V. Mosby, 1975.

Hill, S. D.; McCullum, A. H.; and Scean, A. "Relation of Training in Motor Activity to the Development of Left-Right Directionality in Mentally Retarded Children: Exploratory Study." *Perceptual Motor Skills* 24(1967): 363-366.

Humphrey, J. H. "Comparison of the Use of Active Games and Language Workbook Exercises as Learning Media in the Development of Language Understanding with Third Grade Children." *Perceptual Motor Skills* 19(1964): 627-633.

Johnson, Ronald C., and Gene R. Medinnus. *Child Psychology: Behavior and Development.* New York: John Wiley & Sons, 1974.

Kamii, Constance K., and DeVries, Rheta. "Piaget for Early Education." In *The Preschool in Action* edited by R. K. Parker. New York: Allyn and Bacon, in press

Karpovich, Peter V., and Sinning, Wayne E. *Physiology of Muscular Activity.* Philadelphia: W. B. Saunders, 1971.

Katz, P. A., and Deutsch, M. "Modality of Stimulus Presentation in Series Leaning for Retarded and Normal Readers." *Perceptual Motor Skills* 19(1964): 627-633.

Kennedy, John F. "The Soft America." *Sports Illustrated,* 26 December 1960.

Kephart, Newell C. *The Slow Learner in the Classroom.* Columbus, Ohio: Charles E. Merrill, 1971.

King, Barry G.; Millard, Nellie D.; and Showers, Mary Jane. *Human Anatomy and Physiology.* Philadelphia and London: W. B. Saunders, 1969.

Kirchner, Glenn. *Physical Education for Elementary School Children.* Dubuque, Iowa: Wm. C. Brown, 1974.

Lambert, Hazel M. *Teaching the Kindergarten Child.* New York: Harcourt, Brace and Company, 1958.

Lavatelli, C. *Early Childhood Curriculum—A Piaget Program.* Boston: American Scientific and Engineering, 1970.

Leuba, C. "An Experimental Study of Rivalry in Children." *Journal of Comparative Psychology* 16(1933): 367-378.

Miller, Arthur G., and Whitcomb, Virginia. *Physical Education in the Elementary School Curriculum.* Englewood Cliffs, New Jersey: Prentice-Hall, 1969.

Ministry of Education and Central Office of Information. *Moving and Growing.* London: Her Majesty's Stationary Office, 1952.

Morehouse, Laurence E., and Leonard Gross. *Total Fitness in 30 Minutes a Week.* New York: Simon & Schuster, 1975.

Morgan, Clifford T., and Richard A. King. *Introduction to Psychology.* 5th ed. New York: McGraw-Hill, 1975.

Morris, G. S. Don. *How to Change the Games Children Play.* Minneapolis, Minnesota: Burgess, 1976.

Mosston, Muska. *Developmental Movement.* Columbus, Ohio: Charles E. Merrill, 1965.

Munden, Ivy. *Physical Education for Infants.* London: University of London Press Ltd., 1953.

Painter, Genevieve. *Teach Your Baby.* New York: Simon & Schuster, 1971.

Phillips, John L., Jr. *Origins of Intellect and Piaget's Theory.* San Francisco: W. H. Freeman, 1975.

Piaget, Jean. "Development and Learning." *Journal of Research in Science Teaching.* 2(1964): 176-186.

Piaget, Jean, and Inhelder, Barbel. *The Child's Conception of Space.* New York: Norton, 1967.

Pressey, Sidney L., and Kuhlen, Raymond G. *Psychological Development through Life Span.* New York: Harper and Brothers, 1957.

Prudden Bonnie. *How to Keep Your Child Fit from Birth to Six.* New York, Evanston, London: Harper & Row, 1964.

Read, K. H. *The Nursery School.* 4th ed. Philadelphia: W. B. Saunders, 1966.

Richardson, Hazel A. *Games for the Elementary School Grades.* Minneapolis, Minnesota: Burgess, 1951.

Rosborough, Pearl M. *Physical Fitness and the Child's Reading Problem.* New York: Exposition Press. 1963.

Ryser, Otto E. *A Teacher's Manual for Tumbling and Apparatus Stunts.* Dubuque, Iowa: Wm. C. Brown, 1951.

Schifferes, Justus J. *Healthier Living: A College Textbook in Personal and Community Health.* New York, London, Sydney: John Wiley & Sons, 1970.

Smart, Mollie S., and Smart, Russell C. *Children: Development and Relationships.* New York: Macmillan, 1972.

_____. *Readings in Child Development and Relationships.* New York: Macmillan, 1972.

Sponseller, Doris (ed.). *Play as a Learning Medium.* Washington, D.C.: National Association for the Education of Young Children, 1974.

Sterritt, G. M., and Rudnick, M. "Auditory and Visual Rhythm Perception in Relation to Reading Ability in 4th Grade Boys." *Perceptual Motor Skills* 22(1966): 859-864.

Stuart, Francis R., and Ludlam, John S. *Rhythmic Activities.* Minneapolis, Minnesota: Burgess, 1963.

Travelers Insurance Companies. *Travelers Book of Children's Exercises.* Hartford, Connecticut.

Watson, Robert I., and Henry C. Lindgren. *Psychology of the Child.* 5th ed. New York: John Wiley and Sons. 1973.

Werner, Peter H., and Richard A. Simmons. *Inexpensive Physical Education Equipment for Children.* Minneapolis, Minnesota: Burgess, 1976.

Index

SPECIFIC SKILLS FOR TWO-YEAR-OLDS

SPECIFIC SKILLS FOR FIVE-YEAR-OLDS AND OLDER

SPECIFIC SKILLS FOR CHILDREN AGES SIX TO EIGHT

Refer to listings under "Specific skills for 5-year-olds and older" and expand according to the ability levels of the students.